Ian Gibson was born in Dublin in 1939, and attended Trinity College, Dublin. He lectured in Spanish at The Queen's University, Belfast, and then became Reader in Modern Spanish Literature at London University. In 1975 Ian Gibson left academic life to write full-time. He moved to Madrid in 1978, where he has lived ever since, taking Spanish citizenship in 1984.

Ian Gibson's first book, *The Assassination of Federico García Lorca* (1971), which was immediately banned by the Franco regime, was awarded the Prix International de la Presse. His acclaimed biography, *Federico García Lorca* (1989), won both the Duff Cooper Memorial Prize and the James Tait Black Memorial Prize. Ian Gibson is also the presenter of *Fire in the Blood*, the BBC2 series which celebrates 1992 as the year of Spain, and has written a book to accompany the series.

*Frontispiece*: The River Darro in Granada as seen by David Roberts, 1836.

# Lorca's Granada

## A PRACTICAL GUIDE

*Ian Gibson*

*faber and faber*

LONDON · BOSTON

First published in Great Britain in 1992
by Faber and Faber Limited
3 Queen Square London WC1N 3AU
The Spanish edition first published in 1989
by Plaza y Janés, SA, Barcelona

Phototypeset by Intype, London
Printed in England by Clays Ltd, St Ives Plc

# CONTENTS

# LIST OF ILLUSTRATIONS

# INTRODUCTION
## Federico García Lorca and Granada

Federico García Lorca liked to proclaim that he was from the Kingdom of Granada, often adding for good measure that he had been born, not in the city itself, but in the heart of its fertile river plain, the Vega.

Fuente Vaqueros, the village where the poet came into the world on 5 June 1898, is 18 kilometres from Granada. Lorca spent the first eleven years of his life there and in a nearby village, Asquerosa (today Valderrubio), only moving to the provincial capital with his family in 1909. The Vega was to be his lost paradise and to form the backdrop to all his work. It appears explicitly in many of the early poems and implicitly in the rural tragedies, which draw heavily on the speech, customs and life of this plain, which was lovingly husbanded by the Romans and later, for more than seven centuries, by the Muslims.

Before all else, Lorca was a man of the Granadine Vega. But if his childhood immersion in its ways and rhythms influenced him for life, it is no less true that the city of Granada made a deep impression on his sensibility. It could hardly have been otherwise, given the character and history of the city, and the favourable circumstances – favourable in an artistic and intellectual sense – prevailing there during his adolescence.

Granada is built on several hills and stands at an average height of 2175 feet above sea level. Between it and the Mediterranean – only 48 kilometres away as the crow flies – runs the imposing Sierra Nevada, the highest mountain range in Spain, at the feet of which, along the sea, sub-tropical fruits thrive. Eternal snows, plentiful water, a fertile plain and a burning summer sun: these ingredients make Granada unique.

Before setting out on our first route, it may be useful to look briefly at what Lorca thought about Granada and, in particular, about the fall of this city – the last bastion of Islam in the Peninsula – to the Christians in 1492.

When Ferdinand and Isabella, the so-called 'Catholic Monarchs', overthrew Moorish rule in that year, they promised to respect the property and way of life of Granada's Jews and Moors. But that trust was betrayed – in the case of the Jews, the moment the Christians took possession of the city. They were given a choice: either immediate conversion to Catholicism or banishment. The expulsion order applied not only to the Granadine Jews (of which it seems there were some 20,000) but also to those living in the rest of Spain, who totalled perhaps 500,000 out of a population of 7 million. It has been calculated that half the Jews left the country, the others opting to abjure, become 'New Christians' and remain. Those who went had no choice but to sell their property at rock-bottom prices. Many thousands died in exile in the effort to find a new home.

As for the Muslims, Ferdinand and Isabella went back on their word ten years after the fall of Granada, in 1502. The Moors were now given the same choice as the Jews: become Catholics or leave Spain immediately. Tens of thousands abandoned their homeland, and those who accepted conversion, known pejoratively as *moriscos*, were subject to constant harassment. Finally, in 1609, their descendants were expelled.

Exile, repression, persecution, suspicion: from 1492 onwards these became permanent elements in Spanish life. It is thought that the Inquisition tortured and killed almost a million people. The 'New Christians', crypto-Jews, crypto-Muslims (and, later, Protestants), all went in fear of their lives. The most tolerant country in Europe had become the most intolerant and, perhaps not surprisingly, some of the worst Inquisitors – such as Tomás de Torquemada – were of Jewish extraction.

Lorca identified closely with the victims of such inhumanity. 'I believe that coming from Granada gives me a fellow feeling for all those who are being persecuted,' he said in 1931. 'For the Gypsy, the Black, the Jew . . . for the "*morisco*" all we *granadinos* carry around inside us.'

A few months before his death, the poet was asked for his opinion of the fall of Muslim Granada to the Christians. 'It was a disastrous event,' he replied, 'even though they may say the opposite in the schools. An admirable civilization, and a poetry,

astronomy, architecture and sensitivity unique in the world –
all were lost, to give way to an impoverished, cowed city, a
"miser's paradise", which is currently being stirred up by the
worst bourgeoisie in Spain.' These were strong words, and didn't
help Lorca's chances when the Fascists took Granada in July
1936.

In some of his first poems, written in 1917 and 1918, the
young Federico could not avoid being seduced by the Romantic
vision of Granada, to which foreign writers such as Chateaubri-
and, Washington Irving, Victor Hugo, Théophile Gautier and
Dumas *père* had contributed so signally. But he soon abandoned
this tone, and henceforth the Alhambra and Generalife would
only appear sparingly in his work, and when they did so, freed
from the pseudo-Moorish sentimentality with which earlier
poets had infused them.

As for the poet's scathing reference to the Granadine middle
class, it must be said that he was consistent in this view of his
fellow-citizens. In his letters Lorca returns frequently to the
subject, alleging that the *granadinos* are not genuinely Andalusian but, rather, the philistine descendants of the Christian con-
querors from the north who had resettled the zone and shown
a complete insensitivity to what they found there.

For Lorca, Granada, while set in surroundings of great beauty
(a beauty which the 'worst bourgeoisie in Spain' has done its
best to destroy), is psychologically an enclosed, oppressive city.
He repeatedly said that he felt 'stifled' by the place.

Lorca's feelings about the Granada beneath the surface were
most clearly expressed in his lecture on the Granadine poet
Pedro Soto de Rojas (1585–1658), the title of whose long poem
*Paraíso cerrado para muchos, jardines abiertos para pocos* ('A
Paradise Closed to Many, Gardens Open to Few') he believed
to be the most perfect definition of the true spirit of Granada.
Pondering on the implications of Soto de Rojas's poem, Lorca
came to identify what he called 'the aesthetic of the diminutive'
– the love of small things, the exquisite attention to detail – as
the essence of Granadine art. The local artist (typically, Lorca
assures us, a lonely, reserved creature with few friends) tends
to produce small-scale, carefully wrought work. As examples,

the poet singled out the infinitely subtle glazed tiles of the Alhambra, with their intricate arabesques, and the Virgins made by the sculptor Alonso Cano (1601–67). To these we could add the marquetry and ceramics for which Granada is well known. Little wonder that, for the poet, Granadine sensibility cringes before the 'great cold tower' of the city's Renaissance cathedral which, erected on the site of the Chief Mosque, is a fitting symbol of the defeat of Islam.

Granada, cut off from the sea by the Sierra Nevada, is for Lorca 'full of ideas but lacking in action', preferring to view the world 'through binoculars the wrong way round'. The city's true voice is elegiac in tone, expressing 'the clash of East and West in two palaces, both of them now empty and full of ghosts: the palace of the Emperor Charles V and the Alhambra'.

Writing of the Alhambra, in whose halls he had been fortunate to spend two summers, Richard Ford said in his famous *Handbook for Travellers in Spain and Readers at Home* (1845):

Few *Granadinos* ever go there or understand the all-absorbing interest, the concentrated devotion, which it incites in the stranger. Familiarity has bred in them the contempt with which the Bedouin regards the ruins of Palmyra, insensible to present as to past poetry and romance.

Lorca would have approved of this observation. 'The *granadino* is surrounded by Nature at her most lavish,' he wrote, 'but he never goes out to meet her. The views are staggering, but the *granadino* prefers to look at them from his window.'

The word '*mirador*' is a key term in Granada, and in Lorca's poetry of Granadine inspiration. Literally 'looking-from-place', it can be applied to any of the thousands of vantage-points (gardens, squares, streets) from which, in this hilly city, the most wonderful and unexpected views are obtained. Really, the whole of Granada is a *mirador* and you should make a point of always looking upwards, to catch a view of the Alhambra as you pass a street entrance, or a glimpse of the Picacho de la Veleta high above the city.

Granada is often known in Spain as 'the city of the *carmen*'. The word, Arabic in origin, denotes a hillside villa with an enclosed garden. Granada abounds in *carmens*, particularly in the steep Albaicín quarter across the River Darro from the Alhambra Hill. From the street the gardens are invisible; inside, amid a riot of vines, jasmine, fruit trees and geraniums, splashes the inevitable fountain. Every *carmen* is, or has, a *mirador*. In 1924 Lorca assured a friend that, if he lived in Granada, he could only do so in a *carmen*, 'close to what one feels deeply: the whitewashed wall, the fragrant myrtle, the fountain'. To appreciate Lorca's Granada, one needs to spend at least a few hours in one of these earthly paradises. Such an opportunity is afforded to the visitor by Manuel de Falla's little house, below the Alhambra (Tour Four), although the *carmens* of the Albaicín provide especially impressive views (Sierra Nevada, Silla del Moro, Generalife, Alhambra, valley of the Darro, the city itself, the Vega beyond . . . ). In such an Albaicín *carmen* lives the protagonist of *Doña Rosita the Spinster*, the poet's most poignant incarnation of his vision of Granada.

'Granada has two rivers, eighty belfries, four thousand watercourses, fifty public fountains, a thousand and one jets and a hundred thousand inhabitants,' the poet explained in his lecture 'How a City Sings from November to November'. He forgot to mention the wells of the Albaicín, which in his early work symbolize *la pena*, or the anguish, of this Moorish quarter appropriated by the Christians after the expulsion of its legitimate inhabitants.

And what of the Gypsies of Granada, who until not long ago lived in the caves of the Sacromonte, where they entertained tourists with their wild dancing and singing? We have seen that, in the list of the victimized with whom Lorca claimed to identify as a *granadino*, the Gypsies were at the head. They came to represent for the poet the deepest elements in the Andalusian psyche.

In *cante jondo* ('deep song'), the authentic form of modern flamenco, Lorca found the most profound expression of the Andalusian soul. Since the Gypsies had played a vital role in the development and preservation of the genre, here was an added reason for admiring them. With Manuel de Falla as guide, Lorca, a gifted musician, delved into the origins and nature of *cante jondo*. Out of these explorations came, first, *Poem of Cante*

*Jondo* and, soon afterwards, *Gypsy Ballads*, some of whose landscapes we will recognize in our visit to the Sacromonte and to Granada's version of St Michael's Mount, the Cerro de San Miguel.

Granada can be appallingly hot in July and August. Just before the rigours of the dog-days began in 1928, Lorca expressed the view that the summer is Granada's 'worst hour'. It's impossible not to agree. Granada should be visited preferably in autumn or spring, both of which seasons are in their different ways delightful. The poet himself seems to have preferred the place in autumn, to judge from his letters. Towards the end of September, coinciding with the first rains, Granada recovers its blue sky, almost white during July and August, and takes on a new lease of life. 'Granada is wonderful, full of autumn gold,' Lorca wrote to his friend the musician Angel Barrios in November 1919. 'I've been thinking a lot about you during my walks through the Vega. The colours and melancholy of the place are indescribable.' Two years later another Granadine friend, Melchor Fernández Almagro, received a similar confidence. 'I want to escape from here,' Lorca wrote, 'but not until everything has turned completely golden. The valleys of the Darro and Genil in autumn are the only paths in the world which could lead us to the Country of Nowhere, hidden somewhere up there in the mist.'

In his letters, Lorca often refers to his love for Málaga and longing for the sea. One of the characteristics of Granada, which the poet liked to stress, is its lack of sea, all the more frustrating since the Mediterranean is so close, on the other side of the massive barrier of the Sierra Nevada. For the poet, Granada's separation from the sea has symbolic connotations of deprivation. 'Granada, which sighs for the sea', the city is termed in one of the compositions of *Poem of Cante Jondo*. The poet once observed that, for many people, his 'Sleepwalking Ballad' ('Romance sonámbulo') seemed to express 'Granada's yearning for the sea, the anguish of a city that can't hear the waves and that searches for them in the play of its subterranean water and the undulating mists with which it clothes its hillsides'.

In Lorca's day, getting to the coast was a considerable feat. Nowadays it is much 'nearer' than it was, for a vastly improved road makes it possible to drive to Motril in an hour. None the less the Sierra Nevada, which dominates the city, is a constant reminder that Granada, unlike Seville, is not open to the sea.

This guide would be incomplete if it failed to refer to the Granadine thinker and novelist Angel Ganivet, who committed suicide in 1898, the year in which Lorca was born, at the age of thirty-two. Lorca's generation considered Ganivet one of their masters, and were particularly influenced by his little essay *Granada la bella* ('Granada the Beautiful'), published shortly before his death in 1896. In it Ganivet had expressed his concern about the horrors being perpetrated in the city by the developers. The 'street-widening epidemic', as he termed it, was spreading. Local businessmen were obsessed with the straight line, so utterly at variance with the essence of Granadine sensibility. Ganivet, like Lorca after him, saw that essence in the small, the delicate, the intimate, and dreamt of a Granada in which respect for tradition would be compatible with the demands of modern life. 'My Granada is not that of today,' he wrote at the beginning of his essay, 'but that which could and ought to exist, although I don't know if it ever will.'

The young Lorca and his friends took up Ganivet's challenge and determined to work for a more liberal Granada, more sensitive to the arts, more self-aware. For a Granada that, in accordance with Ganivet's prescription, would preserve the best of the past but live firmly attuned to the times. Lorca once explained that what his generation aspired to was a new, 'universal Granadinism'.

In the prologue to his first book, *Impressions and Landscapes* (1918), Lorca insisted on the primacy of our inner world over the external, and among other recommendations stressed the necessity 'of seeing in empty squares the souls of those who used to cross them'. In preparing this guide I have tried to keep these words in mind. Granada has undergone cruel changes since the poet lived here. The city has grown uncontrollably and garishly, pushing out brutally into the Vega; it is much noisier, much more crowded; it is saturated with traffic. Nevertheless, it is not difficult to reconstruct the poet's city in the imagination, and sometimes we can even come across a corner, unspoilt by the ravages of man and time, which retains rich Lorca associations.

Lorca knew he could not live permanently in Granada, but he liked to return here in summer to renew himself after the hurly-burly of Madrid. Moreover he always said that Granada – Vega and city – had made him the poet he was.

The tours proposed in this guide have been devised to be followed on foot wherever possible. Sometimes, however, a car is necessary. To do them all would take five or six days, and preferably, taking one's time, eight or ten. Nevertheless it is hoped that those Lorca-lovers who cannot stay in Granada for more than two or three days may derive some benefit from what follows, by selecting the routes that most appeal to them.

A word on the plans, taken from the original Spanish edition of this book. These need to be supplemented with the best up-to-date street map of Granada you can find, preferably in advance of your visit but certainly as soon as you arrive in the city. While you're at it, I suggest that you also acquire a good map of the province. When in doubt during a tour, the best rule is to follow the text as closely as possible – or to ask someone the way. You may discover that there are some discrepancies between the *granadino* spelling of street names and standard Castilian ('Calle Almés', for example, should correctly be 'Calle Almez', 'algibe' is the local version of 'aljibe' and so on). Don't worry about this; it's part of being in Andalusia! As regards the street names given in the text, I have usually preferred the spoken to the 'correct' usage, leaving out prepositions and articles when these tend not to be used in normal speech: thus I write 'Calle Reyes Católicos', not 'Calle de los Reyes Católicos', 'Calle Mesones', not 'Calle de Mesones', and so on.

You ought also to equip yourself with a good general guidebook to Granada, since I obviously can't give detailed information about everything of interest in the town (see bibliography).

Finally, a piece of well-intentioned advice. Try if you can to find accommodation on the Alhambra Hill, at least for one night. It is more expensive than down below, in the city proper, but if the money is available you will find it a good investment. To visit Granada in search of García Lorca and not sleep near the Arab palaces, near Falla's *carmen*, would be to miss an unforgettable experience. At the end of the guide I make some suggestions about hotels, pointing out that as a rule it is wise to book a room in advance.

I wish you all joy in Granada, where, thanks mainly to Lorca, I myself have experienced it abundantly.

# TOUR ONE Puerta Real and its Surrounding District

*Length: approximately one hour on foot.*

As I mentioned in the introduction, Lorca was not born in Granada itself but in the village of Fuente Vaqueros, 18 kilometres out into the Vega. While the opening tour could have been designed to take us there, on the principle of first things first, it seems to me that most visitors will want to get their bearings in Granada before exploring the poet's childhood paradise. Perhaps I'm wrong about this, in which case consult Tour Nine.

To begin this tour, find your way to the Puerta Real, the hub of Granada today and yesterday, and with the help of the plan locate the once-handsome building standing between Calles Mesones and Alhóndiga. Its ground floor houses the Gran Café Granada, popularly known as the 'Suizo'. At the time of writing, the Suizo, the most venerable, literary and well-positioned café in Granada, has been closed for several years. (All true lovers of the city are in consternation.) Hopefully it will be reopened under new management, in which case I beg you to have your first breakfast in Granada here, sitting at a table that affords you a view of the Puerta Real. I'm going to take the liberty of supposing that the Suizo has indeed reopened, since I find it too painful to admit to myself that such a place could ever be shut down definitively. The Suizo is undoubtedly one of the great old cafés of Spain, and to my knowledge the only one frequented by Lorca and his friends that still survives.

In 1965, when I began investigating Lorca's assassination, I came here every morning for breakfast and to plan the day's work. At that time the establishment used to provide the most delicious toasted ham rolls I have ever eaten, and the coffee was equally superb. Those breakfasts are unforgettable. In the afternoons I would often return to meet the lawyer and writer Antonio Pérez Funes, a friend of the poet's, and his group of

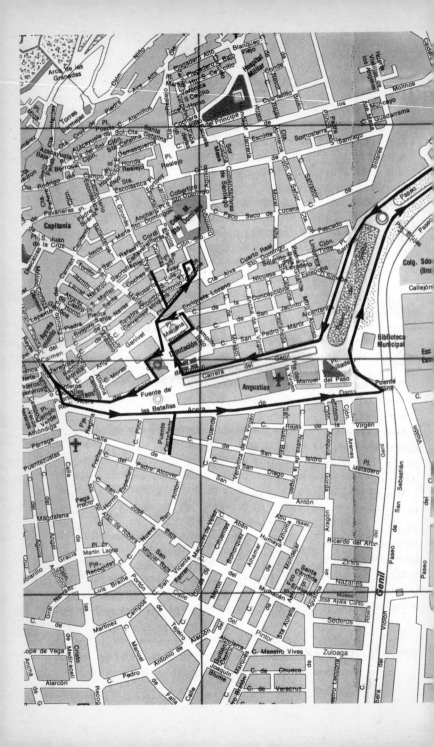

fellow dissidents. Thus began my initiation into the 'things of Granada'. People then were still scared to talk openly about the circumstances surrounding the death of Lorca. Pérez Funes *did* talk, however, keeping his voice down, and gave me information vital for the first steps of my research. You will appreciate my feelings about the Suizo and understand why I want you to enjoy its delights.

Although it may seem difficult to believe, one of Granada's two rivers, the Darro, runs beneath Calle Reyes Católicos and the Puerta Real, turning sharply just outside the Suizo before continuing beneath the Acera del Darro to join the River Genil at the end of the street. Angel Ganivet, mentioned in the introduction, had strong things to say about the covering over of the Darro. In *Granada the Beautiful* he wrote:

I know many cities crossed by rivers great and small from the Seine, the Thames or the Spree to the humble and thirsty Manzanares,* but I've never seen rivers roofed over like our gold-bearing Darro and affirm that the person who conceived the idea of enclosing it within a vault conceived it by night, a night of dire consequences for our city.

When the García Lorca family moved to Granada in 1909 and settled into a rented house on the Acera del Darro, the river still emerged from its tunnel some hundred yards from the Suizo and was crossed a little further down by its last surviving bridge, that of the Virgen de las Angustias (Virgin of the Sorrows). The picturesque scene disappeared for ever just after the Civil War, when the last part of the river was covered.

Why did the Granada authorities go to such lengths to banish the miniscule Darro to invisibility as it traversed the city? The main reason was to tame the beast into which the normally tranquil stream was liable to be transformed when freak cloudbursts broke on the hills where it rises, only 16 kilometres away behind the city. When this happened the river could cause havoc, breaking its banks, flooding surrounding streets and carrying away everything in its path. And so it was that the rat-infested

* Madrid's insignificant and much-maligned river.

Darro was condemned to perpetual darkness as it passed under the streets of Granada.

In 1835 Granadine ingenuity had come up with a '*copla*' (a four-lined snatch of verse) commemorating the tremendous storm of that year, when the river ran amok. The ever-alert Richard Ford recorded it in his *Handbook*:

> Darro tiene prometido
> el casarse con Genil,
> y le ha de llevar en dote
> Plaza Nueva y Zacatín.

This might be rendered:

> The Darro has promised
> To marry the Genil,
> And as dowry will take her
> The Plaza Nueva and Zacatín.

The tunnel begins in the Plaza Nueva, beside the Church of Santa Ana. We'll see its mouth in Tour Five. The narrow Zacatín, a short distance from the Suizo, runs from the animated Plaza de Bib-rambla, parallel to Reyes Católicos, up to the Gran Vía. Before the far-reaching alterations to the town effected during the nineteenth century it was one of Granada's principal streets and bordered the Darro.

The Darro is still capable of rebelling against its imprisonment. In 1951, when after tremendous rains the tunnel was blocked with trees swept down from the hills, the water rose with irresistible strength and burst through the vault in Puerta Real, repeating the river's feat of 1835 and inundating the nearby streets.

It should be added that the Arabic name for the river, Hadarro, gave rise to two forms in Spanish, Darro and Dauro. 'Darro' came to mean, in Granada, *cloaca*, or drain, because the river was just that. 'Dauro' is popularly taken to derive from '*de oro*', since the river is, literally, 'gold-bearing', although it has never produced great quantities of the precious metal. The version 'Darro' prevailed, although the poets of the nineteenth century and then Lorca preferred, understandably, the more 'poetic' Dauro. In his early poems, in his first published prose piece, 'Fantasía simbólica' (1917), and in *Impressions and Landscapes* (1918), the poet refers frequently to the river, particularly to its course behind the city, where it flows down through the lush valley known as Valparaíso, 'Paradise Valley'.

Having mentioned the threat posed to Granada by the Darro, perhaps this is the moment to allude to another, more serious, danger. Granada is the Spanish city most subject to earth tremors, the majority of which, happily, are innocuous and pass unnoticed. During the nineteenth century there were several earthquakes in different parts of the province and more recently, in 1956, a fairly serious one shook the capital itself, causing several deaths and not a little damage to buildings. Many *granadinos* are convinced that one day the jaws of the earth will open and swallow the entire city, Alhambra and Generalife included. It seems that Washington Irving shared this view. In his splendid *Tales of the Alhambra* (1832) (prescribed reading for all lovers of Granada) he mentions a 'long fissure' in the giant Comares Tower in the Alhambra. It showed, he said, that the building 'has been rent by some of the earthquakes which from time to time have thrown Granada into consternation and which, sooner or later, must reduce this crumbling pile to a mere mass of ruin'. The Torre de Comares is still standing, however, more than a hundred and fifty years after the visit of the talented American who, as a child beside the Hudson, had dreamt of the magic of Granada.

But to return to Lorca. In his day there were several other much-frequented cafés in the Puerta Real, which have long since disappeared. On the other side of Calle Mesones, to our left, on the corner of Reyes Católicos, was the Colón (occupying the site of the present Papelería Almacenes Puerta Real); in the Acera del Casino, on the left-hand side of Puerta Real, stood the Casino, of which the poet's father, Federico García Rodríguez, was one of the less staid members (it was notoriously conservative); beside it, on the site occupied today by the Banco Popular Español, was the Imperial, which had a lively terrace on the pavement and was one of Lorca's favourites.

Let's now leave the Suizo, in reality or imagination, and begin

5

our first tour. Turning right and crossing Calle Recogidas we round the corner of the Hotel Victoria and start off down the right side of Puerta Real. In a moment we come to the Librería Continental, one of the best bookshops in Granada, always well supplied with works on the city.

A few doors further down is a bar called Casa Enrique, nicknamed 'El Elefante'. Founded in 1911 and no doubt known to Lorca, this is one of the most agreeable places in Granada for a pre-lunch aperitif and is a favourite with local writers and artists. Mine host, the current Enrique, who took over the business when his father died, provides truly first-rate *tapas*. Introduce yourself and ask him to pour you a glass of *vino de la costa*, the little-known Granada wine (see p. 71).

From the kerb outside Casa Enrique you could make out in Lorca's day the village of La Zubia, where one of the poet's great friends, Francisco Soriano Lapresa, owned property nestling among the lower slopes of the Sierra Nevada. In about 1921 Soriano, Lorca and their fellow members of the group known as the 'Rinconcillo' devised a plan to erect a fake hermitage or shrine in La Zubia on ground ceded by Soriano, the idea being to honour the writer Abentofail and other leading figures of Granadine Islamic culture. Lorca enthused about the view of the proposed folly from Puerta Real, whence it was intended its white dome and little tower would be clearly visible. But, alas, the project never got off the ground. If it had, it would certainly not be visible today from the Puerta Real.

Next door to Casa Enrique is Los Leones, a restaurant founded in 1920 and one of Lorca's favourites. The food is good, the service amiable and the bar at the back pleasant for a chat and a *tapa*.

Continuing on our way down the Puerta Real we cross Calle Pino and soon come to a narrow street, Puente de Castañeda, whose name is a reminder that here was the penultimate bridge over the Darro until it was removed when the last stretch of the river was covered over after the Civil War. At the end of the little street, in the corner house on the right, lived Manuel Fernández Montesinos, the husband of Lorca's sister Concha. When the rising against the Republic began in July 1936, Montesinos had been Socialist Mayor of Granada for eight days. He was arrested immediately and shot on the morning of 16 August 1936, the same day that Lorca was taken into custody.

We are now in the Acera del Darro. On the corner of Puente de Castañeda, at No. 44, is the Hotel Montecarlo, which incorporates the house (No. 46) rented by Lorca's father when the family moved to Granada in 1909. The building was similar to what in England would be termed a terraced house. It had several floors, a vine-shaded patio with a diminutive fountain, and a garden at the end of which stood a small stable with a corral. Geraniums, violets and forget-me-nots abounded, and in the centre of the garden rose a luxurious magnolia. These details are taken from the interesting book on Lorca by his younger brother, Francisco (*In the Green Morning: Memories of Federico*, 1989). Today only the door of the house remains. The rest has been changed beyond recognition.

Francisco García Lorca points out that the family's move to Granada did not mean a complete break with their former life in the Vega. Relatives and friends from Fuente Vaqueros or their second village, Asquerosa, often dropped in; in the ample pantry were heaped fruits and vegetables from Don Federico's estates; every summer the family used to spend several weeks in Asquerosa; and there were always servants from the Vega in attendance.

Among the latter the great favourite was Dolores Cuesta. Illiterate, earthy, good-natured, an inexhaustible fund of country lore, Dolores left an indelible impression on Federico, and her exuberant personality and peasant speech are reflected in the Old Pagan Woman in *Yerma* and the Housekeeper in *Doña Rosita the Spinster*.

In 1916 the family left their house in the Acera del Darro and, after spending a year in a flat in the Gran Vía, moved into splendid accommodation at No. 31 Acera del Casino, across the road from where we are now standing. The handsome building (Plate 1) was pulled down a few years ago and a modern block erected in its place. At the time of writing, the ground floor is occupied by the Banco de Crédito Agrícola. More about the García Lorcas' years there later in this tour.

I suggest that we now continue to the end of the Acera del Darro – a distance of some 300 yards – to see the spot where the underground river is liberated from its prison to merge, normally as a feeble dribble, with Granada's other river, the Genil. The meeting of the waters is not uplifting or sweet-smelling, but I think you should see it.

The Genil, the Singulis of the Romans, is altogether a more substantial river than the Darro. Three hundred and fifty-eight kilometres long, it rises in the Sierra Nevada, crosses the Vega to Loja, proceeds to Puente Genil and Ecija and joins the Guadalquivir at Palma del Río. Just as part of the Darro's water is drawn off behind Granada to supply the fountains and pools of the Alhambra and Generalife, so a large volume of the Genil's is deflected before reaching the city in order to feed the Acequia Gorda, an impressive irrigation channel built by the Muslims and still in perfect working order. It is only in its passage across the Vega that the Genil's stream begins to increase, owing mainly to the contribution of the River Cubillas. The two rivers meet close to Fuente Vaqueros, and Lorca played on their banks as a child.

In one of his best-known poems, 'Baladilla de los tres ríos' ('Little Ballad of the Three Rivers'), Lorca compares Seville and Granada in terms of their rivers. Seville, thanks to the Guadalquivir ('Great River' in Arabic), became Spain's principal port after Columbus's discovery of the New World in 1492. For Lorca, the Guadalquivir is a symbol of freedom, of openness to the world, of love; Granada's rivers, with no boats, suggest frustration and death:

> Para los barcos de vela
> Sevilla tiene un camino;
> por el agua de Granada
> sólo reman los suspiros.

> For the tall ships
> Seville has a road;
> Over the water of Granada
> Row only sighs.

I cannot resist quoting another verse of this poem, with its

8

allusion to the great Giralda Tower in Seville and the pools of still water in the Alhambra and Generalife:

> Guadalquivir, alta torre
> y viento en los naranjales.
> Dauro y Genil, torrecillas
> muertas sobre los estanques.

> Guadalquivir, high tower
> And wind in the orange groves.
> Dauro and Genil, little towers
> Dead over the ponds.

We now cross the street to the attractive Paseo del Salón, which, further on, becomes the Paseo de la Bomba. 'The beauty and fashion congregate on this Alameda, which is constantly injured by overfloodings,' wrote Ford in his *Handbook*. At the end of the century the walk was still fashionable, and the well-off and not so well-off came here each evening to see and be seen. In *Doña Rosita the Spinster* there is an amusing allusion to the social importance of the Salón when the Mother, complaining about her still unmarried daughters, exclaims: 'Our means don't allow us to indulge in the slightest luxury. I often ask them: "Which do you want, my darlings, an egg for lunch or a seat in the Paseo?" And the three of them reply in unison: "Seats"!' Lorca heard the joke from the mother of one of his friends.

On the other side of the Genil is the Piarist Fathers College (Escolapios), where the Granada middle class traditionally sent their sons. Had Lorca's father wanted Federico and Francisco brought up by priests, they would almost certainly have been educated here.

Lorca was a frequent visitor to No. 3 Paseo de la Bomba (just behind the fountain), recently replaced by a hideous block of flats. Here he had two very special friends, the charming dilettante Miguel Cerón Rubio and the Professor of Law at Granada University and MP, the Socialist Fernando de los Ríos, one of the most famous men in the city during the poet's adolescence. De los Ríos took Lorca under his wing and became an intimate friend of the family. Years later Francisco García Lorca married the professor's daughter, Laura.

We return towards the Puerta Real via the Carrera del Genil. A hundred yards up on our left, across the street, is the Church of Our Lady of the Sorrows (Nuestra Señora de las Angustias), finished in 1671. The *granadinos* are devoted to the Virgin, and Lorca was no exception, so have a look inside. The much-venerated image of the Virgin over the main altar was done in the first half of the sixteenth century.

Crossing back to the other side of the street we come in four or five minutes to a small garden in front of the County Council building (Diputación), a seventeenth-century palace whose entrance sports a set of the corkscrew columns so dear to the heart of Spanish baroque. Immediately beyond it is a restaurant and bar, Chikito, which stretches round into the Plaza del Campillo, with its gigantic plane trees. In Lorca's day this was the Café Alameda, where the poet and his group of friends used to meet. They always occupied the same tables in a corner of the café, and as a result the gathering came to be known as the 'Rinconcillo' or 'Little Corner'. It is remembered in a plaque fixed to the façade. José Mora Guarnido, one of the members of the Rinconcillo, conjures up the atmosphere in his book on the poet:

In the morning and until the early part of the afternoon its clients were tough characters from the abattoirs and the fish and general supplies market, chaps 'with hair on their chests', as the silly expression has it, going back and forth on their business; in the afternoon and evening arrived the small-time bullfighters, the flamenco set, the guitarists and singers from the *café chantant* La Montillana, situated nearby, the pimps' chums, the frequenters of La Manigua (the red-light district) and the audience from the Cervantes Theatre opposite, where companies specializing in low-brow entertainment would put on moral operettas for family consumption early in the evening and, late at night, pornographic works for those prudent gentlemen who like from time to time to let their hair down a bit. The odd thing is that, despite such a heterogeneous clientele, the café maintained in permanent session a quintet formed of piano and strings which, every evening until midnight, gave concerts of classical music. And, even more odd, the clientele – contrary to what is often said about the public's ability to appreciate – listened to the concerts with pleasure and respect.*

The high priest of the Rinconcillo was the brilliant and eccentric Francisco ('Paquito') Soriano Lapresa, already mentioned in passing, who had something of the wit, appearance, mannerisms and dubious reputation of a Granadine Oscar Wilde. Soriano possessed a fabulous library, and lent books generously. His collection of erotica was particularly in demand, and it was bruited that his interest in the subject was not merely passive, that strange orgies took place in his house. Other leading lights of the group were the future historian Melchor Fernández Almagro, the painters Manuel Angeles Ortiz and Ismael González de la Serna, the journalist Constantino Ruiz Carnero (who would share Lorca's fate at the beginning of the Civil War), the Arabist José Navarro Pardo, the philologist José Fernández Montesinos and the sculptor Juan Cristóbal.

Visiting Spanish writers and artists not infrequently found their way to the Rinconcillo, which had its heyday between 1915 and, approximately, 1922. There were 'honorary members', such as Manuel de Falla and Fernando de los Ríos, who dropped in from time to time. Foreign writers, musicians and artists passing through town were adopted and taken on privileged tours of secret Granada. Among them were H. G. Wells, Rudyard Kipling, the harpsichordist Wanda Landowska, Artur Rubinstein and the Swedish Hispanist Carl Sam Osberg, who, until he chanced on the Rinconcillo, had wandered around Granada like a lost soul. One day a young Japanese diplomat, Nakayama Koichi, turned up, and José Mora Guarnido records that the *rinconcillistas* pestered him mercilessly about the sexual mores of his compatriots, finding him woefully under-informed on the subject. The Rinconcillo also had its Englishman, a student called Charles Montague Evans, who spent several months in Granada in 1922.

One of the favourite activities of the Rinconcillo was the affixing of commemorative ceramic plaques to the walls of

* José Mora Guarnido, *Federico García Lorca y su mundo* (1958).

houses where famous artists and writers, Granadine and other-wise, had lived. Honoured thus were Théophile Gautier, Isaac Albéniz, the Russian composer Glinka and the seventeenth-century poet Pedro Soto de Rojas. As we will see later, the originals of two of these plaques are still in existence.

If you visit Granada at any season other than winter, it's delightful to sit in the Plaza del Campillo, on the terrace of what was the Café Alameda, and take one's ease. Here Lorca and his friends gathered in the summer, when the Rinconcillo moved out of doors. The four towering planes are the tallest trees in Granada, and it is hoped they will survive the construction of an underground car park being built at the time of writing.

With our backs to the Puerta Real we now make for the right-hand corner of the Plaza del Campillo and enter the Plaza de Mariana Pineda, the young heroine executed in 1833 by the lackeys of the tyrannous Ferdinand VII for the crime of having embroidered a Liberal flag. The statue in her memory was erected in 1841, eight years after the death of Ferdinand. When Lorca arrived in Granada with his parents, the statue reminded him of the folk song about Mariana's sacrifice which he had so often sung with his playmates in Fuente Vaqueros, and which praised her bravery in not supplying the sinister police chief, Pedrosa, with a list of the Liberal conspirators who were plotting against the regime.

Lorca finished a first version of his play *Mariana Pineda* by 1923 but it was not performed until 1927, with sets by Salvador Dalí. On 29 May 1929, just before the poet left for New York, the Catalan actress who had originally produced the play, Margarita Xirgu, put it on in Granada's Teatro Cervantes. It was a great occasion. This distinguished building stood on the edge of the plaza facing the Mariana Pineda statue, and was pulled down in 1966 to give way to the present ugly block.

With the statue on our right we walk straight ahead towards Calle San Matías, and take the street that turns right immediately before it. This is the Cuesta del Progreso, although there is no sign with its name on. Turning immediately left we then enter Calle Varela, which *is* named on the corner. You'll know you're on the right track if you can see the Tower of the Vela at the end of the street, standing on the prow of the Alhambra. At No. 6, on the corner of Calle San Antonio, the premises of a new arts club, the Ateneo Científico, Literario y Artístico de Granada, were opened in 1926. Today the inside of the building has been completely altered.

The Ateneo was founded in opposition to the Centro Artístico, by then a moribund association of geriatric chess-players. Among its promotors were Fernando de los Ríos, Manuel de Falla and Lorca. For several years the Ateneo was one of the most active centres of intellectual life in the city. Lorca gave the inaugural lecture on 13 February 1926, entitled 'The Poetic Image in Don Luis de Góngora'. It was a memorable performance, and the lecture, which the poet later repeated elsewhere, became famous.

Returning to the Cuesta del Progreso we turn left and walk up to the Plaza de los Campos, much changed since pre-war days. On the far side of the square stood the Teatro Isabel la Católica, on the site of the present garage of the same name. The theatre was burnt down by a Republican mob on 10 March 1936 and never rebuilt. Here, on 7 October 1932, the Barraca, the Madrid University touring theatre directed by Lorca, performed Calderón's *Life is a Dream*. In his words of introduction Lorca expressed his emotion at finding himself in the theatre where, as a child, he had seen with astonished eyes some of the classical Spanish works he was now being privileged to resuscitate.

The Ateneo Científico, Literario y Artístico moved in the autumn of 1926 from Calle Varela to premises at the back of the Teatro Cervantes in the Plaza de Mariana Pineda, to which we now return. Here, on 17 October 1926, Lorca gave his lecture on the poet Pedro Soto de Rojas (prescribed reading for his theory of Granada). A few days later, on 28 October, the members of the Ateneo made their way up to the Albaicín where they inaugurated a commemorative plaque on the wall of Soto de Rojas's house. We will see this in Tour Seven. Then, in 1928, Lorca delivered a further two lectures here which showed that he was moving in the direction of Surrealism: 'Imagination,

Inspiration and Escape in Poetry' and 'A Sketch of the New Painting'.

From the Plaza de Mariana Pineda we return to the Plaza del Campillo and enter the Acera del Casino. As was said earlier, the García Lorcas moved to what is now the Banco de Crédito Agrícola, at today's No. 15, in 1916. The fine building (Plate 1), which was pulled down in the 1970s, belonged to the Moreno Agrela family, one of the wealthiest in Granada.

The García Lorcas lived on the second and third floors. The former had two beautiful encased windows and splendid wrought-iron balconies. From the top windows there were glorious views of the Vega and, from the back, Federico could see the Teatro Cervantes and the Plaza de Mariana Pineda.

With Manuel de Falla, Lorca organized a puppet show which took place in this house on 6 January 1923 (Twelfth Night, when Spanish children traditionally get their Christmas presents). The performance proved unforgettable. The programme consisted of the interlude *The Two Talkers*, then still attributed to Cervantes; a tiny puppet play by Lorca, *The Girl who Waters the Pot of Basil and the Inquisitive Prince*, adapted from an old Andalusian story; and the thirteenth-century *Mystery Play of the Three Wise Men*. The musical accompaniments, performed by a small orchestra under the direction of Falla, were elaborate and varied. They included excerpts from Stravinsky's *L'Histoire du soldat* and Albéniz's *La Vega*, Debussy's *Sérénade de la poupée*, a berceuse by Ravel and several early Spanish pieces. Isabel García Lorca, then thirteen, and her ten-year-old friend Laura, daughter of Fernando de los Ríos, sang two songs.

Both Falla and Lorca remembered the occasion with nostalgia years later. Federico had been impressed by the meticulous care with which Don Manuel prepared himself for the occasion. 'In order to amuse some mere children,' he said in 1933, 'he went to the trouble of getting everything absolutely right.'

It's time now, surely, for some light refreshment in the Casa Enrique. If something more substantial is required we can install ourselves in Los Leones which, as pointed out earlier, is one of the few restaurants left in Granada that was frequented by the poet.

TOUR TWO The Heart of Granada

*Length: approximately two hours on foot.*

The Puerta Real is again our starting point. From it we enter the narrow and animated Calle Mesones, beside the Suizo.

A few yards along the right-hand pavement, at No. 12, just after the picturesque old chemist's shop Gálvez, Lorca had an account at Enrique Prieto's bookshop, long since disappeared. At the time of writing the premises are occupied by a children's shoeshop, Nico. The poet made numerous purchases here, as many volumes in the Federico García Lorca Foundation in Madrid attest.

On the other side of the street, some sixty paces further down, at No. 29, was an establishment famous in the annals of the literary life of Granada and important in Lorca's career: Paulino Ventura Traveset's bookshop and printing-house, founded in 1835. The site is currently occupied by the Churrería Alhambra. Ventura Traveset published Angel Ganivet's *Idearium español* in 1897 and, the following year, the first Spanish translation of Washington Irving's *Tales of the Alhambra*. In 1918 Lorca's father provided the money necessary to finance his son's first book, *Impressions and Landscapes*, an account of his travels with Martín Domínguez Berrueta, Professor of the Theory of the Arts at Granada University. It was printed by Ventura Traveset. Ten years later the same house produced the two issues of the avant-garde magazine *gallo* published by Lorca and his friends.

Almost opposite what was Ventura Traveset's we enter a minuscule street called Arco de las Cucharas (Archway of Spoons). The arch was the Arab gateway that stood here on the edge of the Plaza de Bib-rambla. It was demolished at the end of the nineteenth century. At the end of the street, on the right, was the thriving hardware and haberdashery concern owned by Miguel Rosales Vallecillos, whose son Luis played such an

* Plaza de la Libertad de reciente creación

important part in the last days of Lorca's life. The street has another Lorca association, since the stage directions to *Mariana Pineda* indicate that the backdrop to the play's Prologue is the Arab Archway of Spoons – still extant in the heroine's day – framed like a Romantic print with a view of the Plaza de Bibrambla.

The square, the most picturesque in the centre of Granada, is enlivened by flower shops and hums with activity, particularly in the mornings. The young Lorca probably crossed it every day on his way to school and, later, to the university.

We now cross it too, making for the cathedral tower, which we can see looming over the rooftops. The narrow Calle Colegio Catalino, bordered by the archbishop's palace, leads us into the Plaza de las Pasiegas, which is dominated by the main entrance to the cathedral. Lorca disliked the edifice, in his view the negation of the Granadine aesthetic, with its love of the small and the delicate. The Royal Chapel, built before the rest of the cathedral, is, however, one of the most exquisite Gothic churches in Spain. We will visit it later in this tour.

Every Corpus Christi Thursday the poet loved to come to the Plaza de las Pasiegas to see the procession bearing the Holy Sacrament leave the cathedral and begin its course through the streets, always strewn with rose-petals and aromatic herbs for the occasion.

Climbing the steps we turn left and follow the cathedral wall around into the street called Cárcel Baja. A few yards further on there is usually a splendid open-air market specializing in condiments and herbal remedies. Here you'll find the *manzanilla* (camomile) from the Sierra Nevada recommended by the street-crier in *Doña Rosita the Spinster*, cures for dandruff, baldness, 'nerves', diarrhoea, obesity . . . You name the problem, they've got the cure. The spelling and phraseology of the descriptions are primitive and hilarious, the sellers witty and voluble. Don't miss the spectacle.

Opposite the stalls we now enter Calle San Jerónimo, at right-angles to Cárcel Baja. The second street on the left leads us to the diminutive Placeta de Castillejos. Here, at No. 3, was the

17

Colegio del Sagrado Corazón de Jesús, whose headmaster and owner was Joaquín Alemán, a relative of Lorca's mother.

I mentioned in Tour One that, if the poet's father had been a traditional, middle-class *granadino*, he would almost certainly have sent his sons to study with the Piarist Fathers at their college on the other side of the Genil. In fact, Don Federico was a liberal-minded man. He decided, therefore, to entrust them to the good offices of Joaquín Alemán, the Catholic-sounding name of whose establishment was a deliberate misnomer.

The house is today divided into several flats. But the patio is almost as it was, with its eight columns, its little fountain and its basin.

Here Federico and Francisco studied for their *bachillerato* (baccalaureat), attending classes, too, at the official state secondary school a few hundred yards away.

Federico, unlike his brother, was a poor student and the despair of his ex-schoolteacher mother, who was always nagging at him to work harder. Joaquín Alemán told one of his first biographers, Jean-Louis Schonberg (pseudonym of Baron Louis Stinglhamber), that the young Lorca 'did nothing but draw, filling his exercise books with figures and caricatures'. Don Joaquín also remembered that Federico 'was an excellent companion, of easy-going, sweet disposition, almost like a girl'.

As for the teachers, one of them is saved from oblivion in *Doña Rosita the Spinster*. There Martín Scheroff y Aví, who taught literature, appears under his own Christian name as the pathetic Don Martín. According to Francisco García Lorca, Scheroff y Aví had a certain bearing. Already getting on when the brothers entered the college, he was careful to maintain appearances, holding himself erect and dyeing his moustache. He lived alone and, as befitted his profession, entertained literary aspirations, publishing articles and theatre criticism in *El Defensor de Granada*. In Don Martín's complaints towards the end of *Doña Rosita* Lorca recalls the way the rich children attending the Colegio del Sagrado Corazón de Jesús had tormented Scheroff and his colleagues, behaviour which the headmaster was unable to prevent given his need to keep on the right side of his clients.

Walking back to Calle San Jerónimo we turn left and continue down the street to the Plaza de la Universidad. The main entrance to the university, with its two tiers of corkscrew columns, is in the right-hand corner of the square. Lorca studied for two degrees: Law, and Philosophy and Letters. And here he often saw the two professors who were to have most influence on his career: Martín Domínguez Berrueta and Fernando de los Ríos. The building houses only the Law Department today. In 1936 the rear part of the complex was occupied by the Civil Government building,* which overlooked the Botanical Garden and Calle Duquesa. Lorca was kept there for two or three days before being shot. We will visit this part of the university in Tour Six. (If you're in a hurry to see it now, consult p. 98.)

From the Plaza de la Universidad, with its statue of the founder, the Emperor Charles V, we carry on down Calle San Jerónimo. On our left, after the Colegiata (Collegiate Church) of Sts Justo and Pastor, is the sixteenth-century Colegio Mayor (university college) of Sts Bartolomé and Santiago. When the García Lorcas moved to Granada in 1909, the Institute of Secondary Education had no premises of its own and was temporarily housed in this building, which has a handsome courtyard. That autumn, Federico began the second year of his *bachillerato* here (he had done the first in Almería). One of his classmates, José Rodríguez Contreras, later a distinguished specialist in forensic medicine, told me that Lorca was extremely timid to start with, perhaps because he had some sort of complex about being a village boy and was put out of countenance by the greater sophistication of his companions. According to Rodríguez Contreras, one of the masters, a fine specimen of *macho* insensitivity, took a strong dislike to the boy and gave him a bad time. It seems, too, that the young Lorca had to put up with jokes and innuendoes at his expense, and even that he was nicknamed 'Federica' because some of the boys found him effeminate. In the New York poems there are lines that may contain a reference to those harrowing times. In 'Poema doble

* Each province in Spain has a government representative, the Civil Governor, whose offices and residence are housed in the Gobierno Civil.

del lago Eden' ('Double Poem of Lake Eden'), for example, we read:

> Quiero llorar porque me da la gana
> como lloran los niños del último banco,
> porque yo no soy un hombre, ni un poeta, ni una hoja,
> pero sí un pulso herido que ronda las cosas del otro lado.

> I want to weep because I feel like it,
> As the children weep on the dunce's bench,
> Because I'm not a man, nor a poet, nor a leaf,
> But a wounded pulse that probes the things on the other side.

And in 'Infancia y muerte' ('Childhood and Death'):

> Niño vencido del colegio y en el vals de la rosa herida
> asombrado con el alba oscura del vello sobre los muslos
> asombrado con su propio hombre que masticaba tabaco en su
> costado izquierdo.

> Child defeated in school and in the waltz of the wounded rose
> Amazed by the dark dawn of the hair on his thighs,
> Amazed by his own grown-up self chewing tobacco in his left
> side.

Lorca averred that he failed his exams badly several times at the institute. His records show, however, that he did not do nearly so poorly as he liked to make out later. But certainly he was no outstanding student. One of the reasons why he refused to apply himself wholeheartedly at school was that he discovered soon after arriving in Granada that, like so many members of his family on his father's side, he had genuine musical ability, especially as a pianist. Music was to become a consuming passion.

Continuing down Calle San Jerónimo we soon come to Calle San Juan de Dios. Opposite us is the Hospital San Juan de Dios, where Lorca's great-uncle Baldomero García Rodríguez, the black sheep of the García family, died in 1911. Improviser of malicious ditties, expert guitarist and notorious tippler, Baldomero sang, in the words of Federico's mother, 'like an angel'. In 1892 he published in Granada a slim volume of religious and moral verse in which he praised the goodness of God and the beauty of Nature, exhorting the reader to abjure the futile struggle for worldly success. Not surprisingly, Federico revered his unusual great-uncle.

The baroque Church of San Juan de Dios is alongside the hospital, and well worth a visit. It has been magnificently restored and is a dazzling fantasy in gold. We may safely assume that Lorca knew it well. He admired the saint in question – St John of God, today co-patron of the city with the spurious San Cecilio – as we can see from the poem 'Preguntas' ('Questions') in *Book of Poems*.

At the end of the street we come to the Avenida de la Constitución, on the other side of which, behind the Triunfo gardens and fountain, rises the splendid Hospital Real (Royal Hospital), begun in 1511 and finished in 1522. Today it houses the Central Library of Granada University. We cross the street. On our right is an imposing building, now belonging to Granada University. Previously it was a teachers' training college, and here Lorca's mother took her degree. We walk up the Avenida del Hospicio to the entrance to the Hospital Real. I recommend a visit to the handsome library. The university archives are kept here, among them the records pertaining to Federico, Francisco and Isabel García Lorca.

Returning down the Avenida del Hospicio we enter, on our left, the Plaza de la Libertad, inaugurated in 1988 in honour of Mariana Pineda, who was executed here on 25 March 1833, as is recorded on the base of the cross.

The Plaza de la Libertad leads us to the Plaza del Triunfo, at the other side of which rises the twelfth-century Arab gateway known as the Arco de Elvira, mentioned by Lorca in his poem 'Gacela del mercado matutino' ('Ghazal of the Morning Market'):

Por el arco de Elvira
quiero verte pasar,
para saber tu nombre
y ponerme a llorar . . .

Through the gateway of Elvira
I want to see you pass,
To know your name
And start to weep . . .

Calle Elvira, which leads from the gateway to the Plaza
Nueva, was the main street in Granada before the construction
of the Gran Vía at the end of the nineteenth century. In Calle
Elvira live the gaudy Manola girls* of the popular *copla* glossed
by Lorca in *Doña Rosita the Spinster*:

Granada, calle de Elvira,
donde viven las Manolas,
las tres que se van a la Alhambra,
las tres y las cuatro solas.

Granada, Elvira Street,
Where the Manola girls live,
The three who go up to the Alhambra,
The three and the four alone.

On 24 October 1494, two years after Granada fell to the
Catholic Monarchs, the German traveller Hieronymus Münzer
visited the city. One day he went out into the Vega through the
Arco de Elvira. He found that the area immediately beyond
the gate was occupied by an immense Muslim cemetery, and
witnessed a burial after which seven women dressed in white
spread sweet-smelling myrtle branches on the grave. Did Lorca
know a Spanish translation of Münzer's book, originally published in Latin? It is possible that someone may have drawn his
attention to it. And if not he probably knew from other sources
that a Muslim cemetery lay hereabouts. More than two hundred
tombs came to light in 1989 and 1990 during the excavations
for an underground car park, and by the time this book is
published some of them may well be on view to the public.

We now stroll down to the Gran Vía along Calle Tinajilla,

---

* *Manolo, manola* (familiar forms of the Christian names Manual and
Manuela). The word is difficult to explain. It means, more or less, 'flashily
dressed person' and refers to the flamboyant way of dressing popular among
the 'lower orders' in the nineteenth century.

where Martín Domínguez Berrueta, Lorca's arts professor at the university, lived at No. 1. The poet was often entertained here, before Berrueta broke with him following a row over the publication of *Impressions and Landscapes* in 1918.

The Gran Vía de Colón (Columbus Avenue), to give it its full name, was laid down at the expense of numerous buildings of historical and artistic interest, Moorish and later, which were demolished to make way for a suitably 'modern' and 'European' thoroughfare. It was opened in 1901. Granada was riding high at the time on the crest of the sugar-beet boom in the Vega, which made the rapid fortunes of many businessmen, including Lorca's father, and some local wit soon nicknamed the street 'Sugar Avenue'. Lorca said that the Gran Vía had played a major role in deforming the character of his fellow *granadinos*.

While that may or not have been the case, it is only fair to point out that the street was originally more noble than it is now, as can be seen from the buildings from that period still standing, several of which have art nouveau touches and enclosed balconies reminiscent of *fin de siècle* Barcelona.

Turning left we now head up the left-hand pavement of the Gran Vía, passing immediately in front of the present Civil Government building. A few hundred yards later we come to an imposing building at No. 34, which today houses the local delegation of the Andalusian Regional Government. Here, opposite the Monastery of Santa Paula (now about to be converted into a five-star hotel), the García Lorcas lived for a year between 1916 and 1917 after leaving the house at Acera del Darro. On the other side of the street lived an attractive girl, María Luisa Egea, with whom Lorca professed to be in love. María Luisa remained impervious to his timid advances, however, and not long afterwards moved to Madrid.

After another few hundred yards we cross the street to approach the entrance to the cathedral. Before we do so, however, contemplate briefly the monstrous edifice at the end of the Gran Vía. As one might expect, it's a bank – the Bank of Santander to be precise. How, one asks, could such an insult to all things beautiful get planning permission? How could a town council permit such a horror in such a visible place? That the crime was perpetrated is further proof that Lorca and his friends were right in their analysis of the Granadine entrepreneurial mentality.

In front of the building stands a monument to Columbus and Queen Isabella, greenish in hue and therefore almost invisible from the Gran Vía, given the similar colour of the bank's glass encasement. The group is the work of the sculptor Mariano Benlliure. It occupies the site formerly occupied by the Post Office building and a house in pseudo-Moorish style that in Lorca's day was the seat of the Centro Artístico, founded in 1885. Federico joined on 11 March 1915 and left on 1 December 1921. It was here that, according to one version, Fernando de los Ríos, then head of the centre, first met Lorca. Hearing someone playing Beethoven beautifully on the piano downstairs, Don Fernando, a fervent admirer of the composer, had gone to inquire. A conversation ensued and from that moment the law professor took Federico under his wing. Perhaps the momentous meeting took place just where Columbus, on bended knee, is talking to the queen. If not, it must have been near by.

The Centro Artístico had its importance for Lorca and his contemporaries. Here, for example, the painters Manuel Angeles Ortiz and Ismael González de la Serna (who illustrated the cover of Lorca's first book *Impressions and Landscapes*) began to exhibit, as did the sculptor Juan Cristóbal; here Manuel de Falla, Andrés Segovia and Angel Barrios gave concerts and Fernando de los Ríos, Francisco Soriano Lapresa (guru of the Rinconcillo), the philosopher Ortega y Gasset and many others lectured; and here, on 17 March 1918, Lorca read chapters from *Impressions and Landscapes* on the eve of the book's publication.

After this reflection we can visit the Royal Chapel of the cathedral. We enter Calle Oficios through the handsome iron *reja* (grille) which used to protect the entrance to the chapel and which was moved here after the Civil War by Mayor Antonio Gallego Burín, who had been a member of the Rinconcillo and close friend of Lorca. Note the frieze, with the motif of the arms of the Catholic Monarchs, whose initials, F (Ferdinand) and I (Isabella), are repeated throughout.

We continue down Oficios with the south façade of the cathedral on our right and the old Arab university, the Madraza, on our left (the present building is newer, but part of the original is still standing inside).

A few paces further along the street, at the corner of the Calle Estribo, observe the wall of the Royal Chapel, with its later plateresque entrance, its filigree balustrades, profusion of Gothic pinnacles and crockets and handsome stone frieze over the entrance, with the initials of Ferdinand and Isabella alternating.

To the left, at right-angles to the Royal Chapel, is the plateresque Lonja (Exchange). Designed by Enrique Egas, the son of the Brussels architect Jan van der Eycken, it was erected in the mid-sixteenth century, after the Royal Chapel was completed. The Lonja now serves as the entrance to the latter. Once inside note the exceptional *artesonado* ceiling.

The Royal Chapel was begun in 1506, fourteen years after Ferdinand and Isabella took Granada. Isabella, who had died in 1504, was interred provisionally in the Convent of San Francisco, near the Alhambra (we shall visit it in Tour Three). Ferdinand followed her in 1520 and was buried beside her until the chapel was finished in 1521, when the remains of both were reinterred in their final resting place.

The Royal Chapel is truly impressive. You will want to sit down and take your time. The splendid *reja*, which divides it into two, is by the Maestro Bartolomé. 'It is the finest *reja* in Spain,' writes Alfonso Lowe, 'which is to say, in the world.'

The effigies of Ferdinand and Isabella were made in Genoa by Domenico Fancelli and are of Carrara marble. Alongside, by the same sculptor, are those of their daughter Joanna ('the Mad') and her fickle husband Philip the Handsome of Burgundy, son of Maximilian I, the Holy Roman Emperor, whom she had married in 1496. Philip, who ruled for only two years, was the first Hapsburg king of Spain. He died at Burgos in 1506 at the age of twenty-eight leaving his wife broken-hearted. She survived him for nearly fifty years, and died in the convent of Santa Clara at Tordesillas, in Castile, in 1555. All those years she had watched over Philip's coffin, which was taken with hers to Granada.

Note the inscription on the tomb of Ferdinand and Isabella, which reminds us of their role as the scourges of Islam. It begins: 'MAHOMETICE SECTE PROSTRATORES ET HERETICE PERVICACIE EXTINCTORES', 'Overthrowers of the Mahommetan sect and repressors of heretical stubbornness'. As was pointed out in the introduction, Lorca had little respect for the Catholic Monarchs.

He was deeply moved by the sad case of Joanna, however, as can be seen from an early poem, 'Elegy to Joanna the Mad', written in Granada in December 1918 and included in *Book of Poems*. Joanna is one of the first in a long line of unhappy women who appear in Lorca's work, and the poem conveys a strong sense of identification with the victim.

The lead coffins lie in a stark crypt beneath the effigies.

Don't miss the fine retable, which is attributed to Felipe de Vigarni. Unfortunately the steps that lead up to it are roped off, so that one cannot examine it as closely as one would wish.

Of particular interest are the reliefs at the base of the retable, to the right and left of the altar. You will be able to locate them easily if I tell you that the left-hand set are surmounted by a kneeling figure of King Ferdinand, the right-hand by a matching one of Queen Isabella. The two panels on the left, which really form one picture, show the scene in which Boabdil, the last Moorish king of Granada, dismounts from his white charger and proffers the key of the Alhambra to the Christians. The beautifully worked figure on horseback in the foreground of the left-hand panel, clothed in a long robe, is Cardinal Pedro González de Mendoza, known as the 'Third King' of Castile because of his great influence at court. His left, gloved, hand, is open to receive the key. Richard Ford points out that Mendoza's 'pinched aquiline face contrasts with the chubbiness of the king and queen', who ride on his left. The cardinal died three years after the fall of Granada. Behind him and the monarchs are a group of ladies and knights and, in the rear, rows of halberdiers, all splendidly caught. In the right-hand panel, behind Boabdil, pairs of bearded captives emerge in a long row from the Alhambra. There can be no doubt about it: Granada has succumbed.

Ford was enthusiastic about these panels, which he felt confident represented 'the actual scene'. 'Nothing of the kind in Spain can be more curious,' he wrote.

The two reliefs to the right of the altar show the forcible baptism of the Muslims that commenced in 1502. These scenes (men in the left-hand panel, women in the right) look peaceful, yet they were anything but that, as Lorca well knew. As Ferdinand and Isabella had originally sworn to allow the Moors to continue practising their religion unmolested, these reliefs stand as a monument to the duplicity of the Catholic Monarchs. I should perhaps add that they are complemented by the splendid contemporary wood-carvings of the fall of Granada by Rodrigo el Alemán ('Rodrigo the German') in the choirstalls of Toledo Cathedral.

From the Royal Chapel we enter the sacristy, which contains a small but priceless collection of paintings, many of which belonged to Queen Isabella, a great admirer of the Flemish School. Particularly notable are two works by Roger van der Weyden (a *Pietà* and a Nativity), originally part of a triptych (the missing panel is in New York); the exquisite *Prayer in the Garden* by Botticelli; and five marvellous paintings by Hans Memling, among them the deeply emotive *The Virgin with the Dead Christ*. Lorca must have known this collection well and come here with his friends and with Martín Domínguez Berrueta.

As to the poet's feelings about the rest of the cathedral, little need be said. If he disliked its massive external presence, he cannot have had much time either for the vast, cold interior. The fact that the building was raised on the site of the Great Mosque, demolished by the Christians, cannot have been a matter of indifference to him either, believing as he did that the fall of Granada to the Catholic Monarchs had been a disaster.

Refreshment is now probably needed. The remedy is at hand. At No. 14 Oficios, opposite the entrance to the Royal Chapel, is the Bar-Restaurante Sevilla, a famous establishment in Granada and one of the few surviving restaurants from pre-war days.

An episode that was often recounted by Lorca's friend the poet
and literary scholar Dámaso Alonso occurred here. It happened
in 1927, just after Lorca and other poets of his generation had
been in Seville to celebrate the third centenary of the death of
Luis de Góngora. One night Federico invited Alonso, who was
visiting Granada with his mother, to dine with him in the Sevilla.
No sooner had they sat down than Lorca called the waiter and
asked for 'Las Soledades'. Dámaso Alonso thought that this was
some house speciality or local wine, but to his amazement the
waiter began to recite Góngora's highly complex poem, the
*Primera Soledad*. A few days earlier, Alonso, the leading
authority in Spain on Góngora, had performed in Seville the
amazing feat of reciting the entire poem from memory, all 1091
lines of it. Now Federico had shown him that he had a competi-
tor. Alonso couldn't believe his ears. The 'waiter' turned out to
be the owner of the restaurant, a good friend of Lorca and a
fervent admirer of Góngora.

The Sevilla, as well as retaining its reputation as an excellent
restaurant, always has on offer a range of first-rate *tapas*. The
present owner, Juan Luis Alvarez, is the nephew of the reciter
of Góngora, and is a fund of information on things Granadine.
If he is on the premises you should make his acquaintance. The
little terrace is ideal for dining, moreover, and provides a relaxed
view of the wall of the Royal Chapel.

Just below the Sevilla is the Alcaicería, in Moorish times a
silk market. The building was burnt down in 1843 and the
present reconstruction has little or nothing to do with the original, being a mere pastiche.

We walk down the tiny Calle de la Alcaicería, at the very end
of Oficios on the left, crossing the attractive Zacatín – the street
that, in the *copla* quoted in Tour One, the turbulent Darro
promises to sweep down as dowry to the Genil – and enter
Calle López Rubio. On the right is Calle Tundidores (Cloth-
Shearers Street), where Lorca's mother, Vicenta Lorca Romero,
lived between 1881 and 1882.

Carrying straight on we cross the ugly Calle Reyes Católicos
(the Darro is beneath our feet) and enter another tiny street

whose name, Puente de Carbón, reminds us that here, before the river was vaulted over, there was a bridge.

On the left-hand side of the street is the Bar Jandilla, which has been boarded up for several years now. It was frequented before and during the Civil War by Commandant José Valdés Guzmán, the first Civil Governor of Granada after the rebels took the city in July 1936 and perhaps the person most responsible for Lorca's death.

At the end of the street is the Moorish Corral del Carbón, built in the fourteenth century as a public granary. You should have a look inside, for this is the only building of its kind in Granada, and, indeed, in Spain.

Proceeding down Calle Mariana Pineda we take the first street on the left, Lepanto, and enter, straight ahead, the diminutive Placeta de Gamboa. Turning left, we find ourselves in Escudo del Carmen. At No. 8, four or five doors down on the left (Bolsos Pliego at my last visit) lived Lorca's piano and composition teacher, Antonio Segura Mesa, who had a profound effect on his development.

Segura had been born in Granada in 1842, and was therefore already elderly when Lorca became his pupil. A shy, retiring man, he had dreamt in his youth of being a great composer in the line of Verdi, but, alas, the dream had never come true. He succeeded in composing an opera of Biblical inspiration, *The Daughters of Jephthah*, certainly, but it seems that it was booed off the stage during its première. Don Martín in *Doña Rosita the Spinster* incorporates several details from Segura's career, amongst them this opera, now converted into a play called *The Daughter* (not *Daughters*) *of Jephthah*. Segura, a competent pianist, also composed music for *zarzuelas* (lighthearted operettas) and, before Lorca came his way, had taught two outstanding Granada musicians: Angel Barrios and Paco Alonso.

Federico revered the old teacher who, as well as stimulating his innate musical talent and ensuring that he acquired an excellent piano technique and solid knowledge of harmony, took him into his confidence and recounted the ups and downs of his life as a less-than-successful composer. 'The fact that I haven't reached the stars doesn't mean that the stars don't exist,' he would chuckle, and Lorca never tired of repeating this phrase to his friends, if we are to believe his biographer José Mora Guarnido.

The poet was deeply upset by the death of Don Antonio, who had encouraged him to become a professional musician, and when, two years later, he published his first book, *Impressions and Landscapes*, it was passionately inscribed to his memory.

Antonio Segura gave Federico his classes in the García Lorcas' house on the Acera del Darro. As we make our way back down Escudo del Carmen we are almost certainly following his footsteps. In a few moments we arrive in the Plaza del Carmen, seat of the Granada Town Hall (Ayuntamiento). On the afternoon of 20 July 1936, the rebels installed a battery opposite the building and arrested all the left-wing councillors they found inside, among them Lorca's brother-in-law Manuel Fernández Montesinos, the Socialist mayor. They were taken to the Provincial Prison, on the outskirts of the city on the road to Jaén and the majority of them, including Fernández Montesinos, were executed soon afterwards.

Opposite the Town Hall, on the corner of the continuation of Escudo del Carmen, is the Club Taurino. Before the war this was the Café Royal, a conservative stronghold. It was burnt by the 'Reds' during the disturbances of March 1936.

Behind the Club Taurino, in Calle Zaragoza, there is a famous restaurant, Los Manueles, which is a positive institution in Granada. The place is very picturesque, the menu includes Granadine specialities, at the bar they serve appetizing *tapas* and among the waiters there is even a poet, José Gallart, a true local character.

From the continuation of Escudo del Carmen, how would Antonio Segura Mesa have proceeded to the García Lorcas' house in the Acera del Darro? Did he always follow the same route? I can't say. It's difficult to imagine, at all events, that such a serious and timid man would have wished to take a short cut by traversing the red-light district of La Manigua to his left (destroyed by the Franco authorities). Probably, therefore, he carried straight on to the Acera del Casino.

Calle Ganivet, to which we now descend by the steps at the

end of Escudo del Carmen, did not exist then. It was built after the war. The authorities could hardly have chosen a worse name to give to this unbeautiful street than that of Ganivet, the passionate lover of Granada and enemy of the town's moderniz-ers. Crossing it to the left we continue for 25 yards under the arcade and come to Almona del Campillo, which leads down to the Acera del Casino. The street was renamed Comandante Valdés after the war, reverting to its original identity with the arrival of democracy.

Once again we are back in the Puerta Real.

# TOUR THREE  The Alhambra and Generalife

*Length: approximately three hours on foot. If you don't feel energetic enough to climb the steep hill to the palaces (a walk not to be missed if at all possible), you can drive up to the car park via the Cuesta de Gomérez, hop on a bus or use a taxi. Since 1991 visitors are no longer allowed to take their cars into the Alhambra precinct unless staying at the Parador San Francisco or Hotel América. In 1993 a new access road to the Alhambra, compulsory for all traffic, will be opened. Starting 1 kilometre out along the road to the Sierra Nevada, it will lead up to the huge car park behind the Alhambra. The time-hallowed access to the palaces via the Cuesta de Gomérez will then be closed to all vehicles except (I am told) a small, non-polluting and almost certainly electric bus. Freed from the exhaust fumes that have almost destroyed it, and the cruel din of engines, the Alhambra Wood will soon recover its former silence and glorious leafage. All praise to those who for many years have worked to make this miracle possible.*

Several streets, roads and alleyways lead up to the Alhambra (in Arabic, the Red Castle), but I suggest we take the classic route up the steep Cuesta de Gomérez, which begins in the Plaza Nueva.

The hill is flanked, in its lower reaches, by shops specializing in *taracea*, marquetry work – an expression of the love of the small and the delicate that Lorca identified as characteristic of the Granadine artistic temperament.

In the Cuesta de Gomérez lived the two saints who have left the most permanent mark on Granada: John of God (1495–1550) and John of the Cross (1542–91). Both lodged in the once noble house standing on the left of the street immediately before the Puerta (or Arco) de las Granadas, 'The Gateway of the Pomegranates', which bestrides the hill just ahead of us. Here St John of God founded a hospital and St John of the

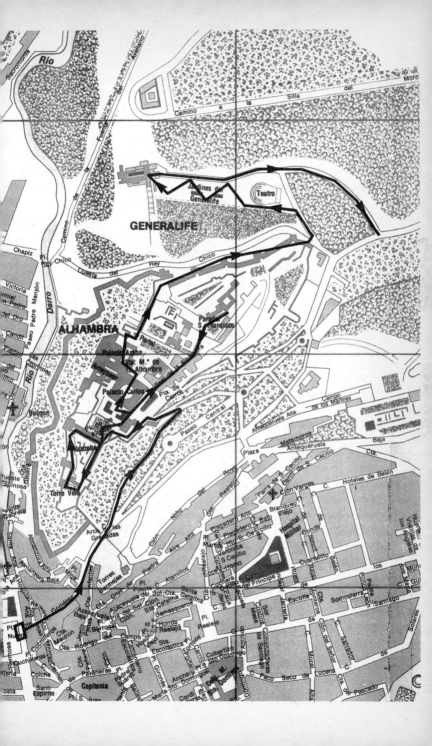

Cross stayed until the builders finished the Carmelite Convent, higher up the hill, of which he was to be prior from 1582–8. Lorca admired both saints, John of God for his good works (see p. 21) and sweetness of temperament, and John of the Cross as a poet.

The Puerta de las Granadas is the work of the architect and painter Pedro Machuca, a disciple of Michelangelo, and was built about 1546 in pure Renaissance style. It is surmounted by the imperial shield of Charles V: note the two-headed Hapsburg eagle and the three stone pomegranates which give the gateway its name.

Perhaps this is the moment to comment briefly on the name Granada. It derives from an ancient Iberian place-name, Garnata or Granata, which, contrary to popular supposition over the centuries, has nothing to do with the word for pomegranate in Spanish, *granada*. The fact that the words coincided, and that the pomegranate later came to abound in these parts, made the choice of the fruit as emblem of the city an obvious one.

Garnata was originally an outlying quarter of an earlier Iberian town, Iliberri, situated on the hill known since Muslim times as the Albaicín (which we shall visit in Tour Five). When the Muslims decided to build on what is today the Alhambra Hill, they retained the indigenous name of the district.

The Puerta de las Granadas marks the transition between the town and the Alhambra Wood, between prose and poetry. It has been suggested that Lorca's 'Romance sonámbulo' ('Sleepwalking Ballad') owes part of its inspiration to the wood, whose greenness and freshness are so striking after the glare and heat of the lower town:

Verde que te quiero verde.
Verde viento, verdes ramas.
El barco sobre la mar
y el caballo en la montaña . . .

Green how I love you deeply green.
Green wind, green branches.
The boat out on the sea
And the horse on the mountain . . .

34

Numerous writers, Spanish and foreign, have attempted to convey in words the magic of this wood. No one did it better, in my opinion, than Théophile Gautier – an author much admired by Lorca and his friends – who arrived in Granada in 1843. Gautier describes (in his *Voyage en Espagne*) the path we're about to take up the hill, to the left of the main avenue, and notes the abundance of water that characterizes the place:

The noise of the babbling water mingles with the hoarse buzzing of a hundred thousand cicadas or crickets whose music never stops and which brings one's ideas back forcibly, despite the coolness of the spot, to the torrid South. The water gushes out on all sides, from under the tree-trunks and through the cracks in the old walls. And the hotter the weather the more the springs well up, for they are fed by the melting snow. This mixture of water, snow and fire makes Granada's climate unique in the world, a true earthly paradise.

Bravo! I would suggest, however, that it is in the silence of night that the water of the Alhambra Wood comes fully into its own, rushing down the hillside beside the paths, bubbling and splashing in subterranean conduits. Doubtless the Seville poet Manuel Machado was thinking of the latter when he defined the true personality of Granada as '*agua oculta que llora*', 'hidden water that weeps'. Weeps for what? I imagine he was alluding to 1492, to the persecution and definitive exile of Granada's rightful inhabitants. Do make a point of lingering here by night (preferably accompanied, just in case): I am sure you will find the experience unforgettable.

Before setting off up the hill we should cross the street briefly to glance at a plaque set into the wall just behind the Puerta de las Granadas. This reproduces a tribute to the Alhambra by the Almerian poet Francisco de Villaespesa (1877–1936), famous in his day but now almost completely forgotten. In 1911 the young Lorca was at the première of Villaespesa's verse play *El alcázar de las perlas* ('The Castle of Pearls') in the Isabel la Católica Theatre, whose site we saw in Tour One. The theme of the play is the mythical origin of the Alhambra, and some of its lines, such as the song about Granada's fountains, were great hits with the audience:

Las fuentes de Granada . . .
¿Habéis sentido
en la noche de estrellas perfumada,
algo mas doloroso que su triste gemido?
Todo reposa en vago encantamiento
en la plata flúida de la luna . . .

The fountains of Granada . . .
Have you ever heard,
In the perfumed, starry night,
Anything more sorrowful than their sad moan?
All reposes in a vague enchantment
In the fluid silver of the moon . . .

Villaespesa declared that it had been his aim to write the
tragedy as it might have been composed by 'a Granadine Arab'.
The phrase, which today seems ridiculous, shows to what an
extent the literary atmosphere of the town was still pervaded
during Lorca's adolescence by a sickly pseudo-orientalism. As I
said in the introduction, the poet could not avoid being affected
by the fashion, but after his first efforts in the genre soon
desisted.

A word on the famous elms of the Alhambra Wood, now in
mortal danger from Dutch elm disease. It has been repeated *ad
nauseam* that they were planted by one of the Dukes of Wellington, who owned the extensive estate in the Vega, the Soto de
Roma, on which Lorca was born. But the fact is that neither
the Iron Duke, who never visited his estate, nor his successors
had anything to do with the trees.

Returning now to the left of the main avenue and beginning
our ascent up the steep path ahead of us (there are stone benches
for resting), we pass the cross that gives this its name, the Cuesta
de la Cruz (Hill of the Cross). In a few minutes we come to
the monumental Pilar de Carlos V (Charles V's Fountain), a
masterpiece of its kind. It was designed in 1545 by Pedro
Machuca, who built the Puerta de las Granadas and the Palace
of Charles V. The three mythological heads from whose mouths
the water falls into the basin represent, according to some
authorities, Summer, Spring and Autumn, to others Granada's

three rivers, the Darro, Genil and Beiro (a phantom river that descends to the Vega from the Sierra de Víznar and is normally without a drop of water). The fountain is flanked at both ends by the heraldic shield of Don Iñigo López de Mendoza, the second Count of Tendilla and first Marquis of Mondéjar, Governor of the Alhambra at the time Machuca was working in Granada. The work is surmounted, like the Puerta de las Granadas, by the imperial shield of Charles V.

My main reason for mentioning the Pilar de Carlos V is that Lorca often came here, his presence on one occasion being immortalized in an interesting photograph (Plate 4a). The poet seated himself immediately below the central mask (the Genil or Spring, take your pick), under the Latin inscription that proclaims grandly: 'IMPERATORI CAESARI KAROLO QUINTO HISPANIARUM REGI', that is, '[Erected by] the Emperor Charles V, King of the Spains'. You may want to sit in exactly the place chosen by Lorca, although, now that the fountain is working again after having been dry for many years, this may involve getting a bit wet.

We now make our way, behind the Pilar de Carlos V, up to the massive Puerta de la Justicia (Gateway of Justice), finished in 1348 by Yussuf I and called by the Muslims Bib Axarea, the Gateway of the Esplanade. Of the two current entrances to the Alhambra, it is by far the most impressive.

Note the marble keystone of the great horseshoe arch, with its enigmatic sculpted hand. This has been interpreted variously. For some authorities it is an amulet warding off the evil eye; for others an emblem of the Koran, the five fingers corresponding to the fundamental precepts of the law: unity of God, prayer, fasting, alms and pilgrimage to Mecca.

Emerging from the gateway, whose twists are skilfully designed to hinder the entrance of an enemy force, we find ourselves in a narrow alleyway leading gently upwards. At the end, on the right, is the Puerta del Vino (Gateway of the Wine), made famous by Debussy's prelude of this name, as a ceramic plaque placed alongside reminds us. Debussy had never been in Granada, and 'La Puerta del Vino', which Lorca calls in a letter 'the impossible dream' of the French composer, was inspired by a picture postcard. Like an earlier work, 'La Soirée dans Grenade', published in 1903, it has the rhythm of an *habanera*.

Manuel de Falla had become friendly with Debussy in Paris and no doubt told Lorca about their relationship. The poet loved Debussy's music deeply, and several of his compositions were in his repertoire. In his lecture on *cante jondo* or 'deep song' (authentic flamenco), delivered in Granada in 1922, Lorca claimed that 'La Soirée dans Grenade' captures to perfection the atmosphere of nocturnal Granada, with 'the far-off blue of the Vega, the Sierra saluting the tremulous Mediterranean, the huge spears of mist jabbing the distances, the town's admirable *rubato* and the delirious games played by the underground water'. This may be something of an exaggeration, but one thing is certain: all true lovers of Lorca and Falla will make a point of familiarizing themselves with Debussy's 'Granadine' music.

The Catalan Isaac Albéniz was another composer-pianist enamoured of Granada, which had inspired many of his works. As a young man he had fallen in love with the daughter of the curator of the Alhambra and, in 1908, aged forty-eight, told Falla in Paris that his only dream was to return to Granada and settle down there. But he died a year later with that dream unfulfilled. Lorca and his friends in the Rinconcillo admired Albéniz, and when the poet was in Barcelona in 1935 he visited his grave and composed a fine sonnet in his honour. José Mora Guarnido has recalled the occasion on which the Rinconcillo placed a ceramic plaque in memory of Albéniz on the wall of the Casa del Arquitecto (the curator's house in the Alhambra). This house was later destroyed, the present administrative building on the other side of the Puerta del Vino taking its place. The plaque was then replaced. It reads: 'To Isaac Albéniz, who lived in the Alhambra. Spring 1882'.

Beside the Puerta del Vino, flanked by the Quebrada and Homenaje towers of the Alcazaba, stretches the Plaza de los Aljibes (Square of the Wells) where the Cante Jondo Competition was held on 13 and 14 June 1922. The competition was organized, with Arts Centre and Town Council backing, by Manuel de Falla and a numerous team of helpers that included

Miguel Cerón, José Mora Guarnido, Lorca and many other members of the Rinconcillo.

The plaza was decorated by the Basque painter Ignacio Zuloaga and on both nights a huge and gaily dressed audience packed the precinct to bursting point. Among the numerous foreigners present was John B. Trend, later the first Professor of Spanish at Cambridge. Trend had become a close friend of Falla following his initial visit to the composer in 1919. When he got back to London he published an account of those two memorable evenings (on the second of which there had been a downpour). 'Wherever one looked there were exquisite figures in gay, flowered shawls and high combs,' he wrote in the *Nation and the Athenaeum*, 'while many had put on the silks and satins of bygone days, and appeared in the fashion of the thirties and forties – the Spain of Prosper Mérimée and Théophile Gautier, of Borrow and of Ford.'

The great surprise of the competition was the performance of Diego Bermúdez Calas, 'el Tenazas' ('Pincers'), an old singer, almost forgotten, who, it was said, had walked to Granada all the way from Puente Genil, in the province of Córdoba, a cross-country hike of some 130 kilometres. Bermúdez sang the first night with great power and carried all before him.

Another prize-winner was the eleven-year-old Manuel Ortega, 'el Caracol' ('The Snail'), destined to become one of the most outstanding flamenco singers of the century.

Falla was scandalized by the fact that the competition left in its aftermath an ugly discussion about what should be done with the profits that had accrued as a result of the venture's success. The punctilious composer decided that he had had enough, and withdrew to his house.

The competition, with the further insights it afforded Lorca into the flamenco tradition, confirmed the broadly Andalusian direction of his work at this time. His *Poem of Deep Song*, largely composed during the preparations for the exciting event, led, before long, to the *Gypsy Ballads*.

Recent excavations have reduced the dimensions of the northern side of the Plaza de los Aljibes. Previously the visitor could stroll to the edge of the walls, or stand on the *cubo* (bastion) situated below the Torre del Homenaje. From this vantage-point there were fabulous views of the Albaicín quarter opposite. Falla, Lorca and their friends often went there. One autumn day in 1921, as he looked out over the Vega, Lorca suddenly had the feeling that the plain was a 'submerged bay'. 'Standing on the *cubo*, have you never had an urge to embark?' he wrote to his friend Melchor Fernández Almagro. 'Have you not seen the boats bobbing at the foot of the towers? Today I realize, in this grey and mother-of-pearl twilight, that I am an inhabitant of a marvellous Lost Atlantis.'

From the *cubo*, as from other points along the walls of the Alhambra, the view of the Albaicín at night is startling. 'Below lies Granada,' writes Ford, 'with its busy hum, and the lights sparkle like stars on the obscure Albaicín as if we were looking *down* on the reversed firmament.' Ford must have heard that the phenomenon was known to locals as the *'Cielo Bajo'* or 'Low Sky', a title which Lorca almost gave to one of his collections of verse, finally preferring *Suites*.

At the beginning of the Civil War, the Nationalist rebels installed a cannon on the *cubo*, firing across the Darro valley at the Republican loyalists entrenched in the Albaicín. From such a position it was impossible to miss.

Towards the northern edge of the square is a kiosk, built around the well that until not long ago supplied visitors with a glass of cool water mixed, if one wished, with a drop of aniseed. For hundreds of years there has been a well here. Its water, according to Théophile Gautier in 1843, was 'clear as a diamond'. Alas, the huge reservoir under the plaza is now empty and we can no longer imitate Lorca and the painter Manuel Angeles Ortiz, who posed here together for a photograph in 1924 with a glass of the celebrated water in their hands.

What other Lorca associations are conjured up by the Plaza de los Aljibes? Certainly he would have been aware of the feat performed by the invalid soldier José García, recorded in a plaque, who 'at the risk of losing his life saved from certain destruction the castles and towers of the Alhambra in 1812'. Before abandoning the Alhambra, which they had converted into a barracks, Napoleon's troops, under the command of

Sebastiani, blew up several towers and mined the rest. The said José García foiled their plans by managing to defuse the explosives. That, at least, is the story.

From the Plaza de los Aljibes there is a fine view of the façade of the Palace of Charles V. The building was designed, as has been said, by Pedro Machuca.

The emperor had fallen in love with Granada during his honeymoon here in 1526 with the beautiful Isabella of Portugal, and the idea came to him of erecting within the Alhambra a splendid Christian palace to vie with the Muslim constructions. Work began the following year. A glance at the façade of the unfinished building suffices to grasp the symbolic message intended. Nothing could be more unlike the delicacy of the Alhambra's halls and patios. Built of massive blocks of yellowish stone, the edifice speaks eloquently of power and conquest. For Lorca, as was mentioned in the introduction, the juxtaposition of the Palace of Charles V and the Alhambra expresses a constant struggle to the death being fought inside the mind of every *granadino*: a struggle between East and West, the oriental and the occidental.

Since the nineteenth century a virulent polemic has been raging over this building. The Romantics, understandably, considered it outrageous, an insult to the Moorish palaces and a vivid reminder of the destruction of a civilization. Richard Ford and Théophile Gautier took a sensible line on the matter. They allowed that the pile has its own beauty, but maintained that it had been erected in absolutely the wrong place.

In 1889 a great celebration took place in the Palace of Charles V. This was the crowning, with due pomp and ceremony, of the Valladolid poet José Zorrilla as the 'National Bard' of Spain. Zorrilla's stay in Granada gave rise to many anecdotes. One of them is still recounted gleefully in the town. According to this, the poet went to pawn his gold crown when he returned to Madrid, discovering to his chagrin that it was no more than a cheap imitation. The story, while it may have no basis in fact, confirms what is generally believed about the *granadinos*, namely, that they are penny-pinching. Lorca shared this view.

Zorrilla had written numerous compositions of Granadine

inspiration. Lorca, born nine years after the celebration in the Palace of Charles V, knew at least some of these and in one of his first publications, 'Fantasía simbólica' (1917), referred to Zorrilla's love of the city, comparing it in intensity to Angel Ganivet's.

Before entering the Alhambra I suggest that mentally we prepare ourselves further by climbing the Torre de la Vela, which stands on the prow of the Alcazaba looking out over the city and the Vega beyond. The entrance ticket, as for the rest of the Alhambra and the Generalife, can be acquired in the office beside the Puerta del Vino.

The Vela is one of the most famous symbols of Granada. A well-known *copla* expresses the love that the *granadinos* feel for this watchtower whose great bell regulated, until quite recently, the use of the irrigation channels in the Vega:

> Quiero vivir en Granada
> solamente por oír
> la campana de la Vela
> cuando me voy a dormir.

> I want to live in Granada
> Only to be able to hear
> The bell of the Vela
> When I lie down to sleep.

Lorca glossed this verse in the poem entitled 'Del amor que no se deja ver' ('The Love Which Won't Reveal Itself'), included in *Diván del Tamarit*.

On the evening of every 1 January and throughout 2 January the Vela bell tolls out to remind the *granadinos* that it was on 2 January 1492 that the city surrendered to the Christians and the pennant of St James and Cardinal Mendoza's cross were hoisted on the highest point of this tower.

Every 1 and 2 January the *granadinos* flock here to celebrate the event, and it is believed that any girl who rings the bell will marry before the end of the year.

In summer it's preferable to climb the tower in the early morning or late afternoon, because the heat on top can be tremendous.

Close to the entrance to the tower is a plaque with a celebrated quotation from the Mexican poet Francisco A. de Icaza. It reads 'Dale limosna, mujer, que no hay en la vida nada como la pena de ser ciego en Granada', that is, 'Give him alms, woman, for nothing in life is worse than being blind in Granada'. The view from the top of the Vela will convince you that Icaza was right – if you still need convincing, that is.

Richard Ford often came up here when he was living in the Alhambra, and there is an unsurpassable description of the view in his *Handbook* which I feel it my absolute obligation to quote:

Below lies Granada, belted with plantations; beyond expands the Vega, about 30 miles in length by 25 in width, and guarded like an Eden by a wall of mountains. The basin was once a lake, through which the Genil burst a way at Loja. The Vega is studded with villages and villas; every field has its battle, every rivulet its ballad. It is a scene for painters to sketch, and for poets to describe. To the l. rise the snowy Alpujarras,* then the distant Sierra of Alhama, then the round mountain of Parapanda, which is the barometer of the Vega; for when its head is bonneted with mists, so surely does rain fall: *'Cuando Parapanda se pone la montera, Llueve aunque Dios no lo quisiera'*. Nearer Granada is the *Sierra de Elvira*, the site of old Illiberis [*sic*]† and below the dark woods of the *Soto de Roma*. To the r. is the rocky defile of Moclín, and the distant chains of Jaén. The *Torre de la Vela* was gutted by the French. It is so called, because on this '*watch*-tower' is a silver-tongued bell, which, struck by the warder at certain times, is the primitive clock that gives notice to irrigators below. It is heard on a still night even in Loja, 30 miles off. Ascend it also just before the sun sets, to see what is his glory in these southern latitudes, when he crimsons heaven and earth. Then as darkness comes on, the long lines of burning weeds and stubble in the Vega run and sparkle, crackling like the battle flashes of infantry; and, as the old warder never fails, and justly, to remark, recall the last campaigns of the Moor and Christian. Then in the short twilight how large the city below looms, always a grand sight from an elevation, but now growing in mystery

---

* The Alpujarras are, in reality, on the other side of the Sierra Nevada peaks visible from Granada.

† There has been much debate about the exact site of ancient Iliberri. Ford's assumption is no longer feasible (see p. 75).

and interest in the blue vapours. How Turner would paint it! and then the busy beelike distant hum of life!

Today, alas, the scene has changed dramatically for the worse. Until the 1950s the last streets of the city merged almost imperceptibly with the orchards, villas, farms and fields of the Vega. Then speculation, unchecked by municipal strictures, ran amok and the city began to invade the plain. Huge new blocks were thrown up and the hitherto small bypass, the Camino de Ronda, running between the city and the Vega, was widened. The results are all too obvious from the Alhambra Hill.

Walking back now to the Plaza de los Aljibes, I want to suggest that, before entering the Alhambra, we visit the church standing to the right of the Palace of Charles V, and the little street on to which it opens.

The church, Santa María de la Alhambra, finished in 1617, was built on the site of the Great Royal Mosque, not a vestige of which remains above ground.

The church has a fascinating Lorca connection. In 1929 the Brotherhood of Santa María de la Alhambra organized its first Holy Week procession, for the night of 27 March. A few moments before the procession left the church, an unexpected problem arose: someone had arrived from Madrid with the express purpose of fulfilling a vow to the Virgin, by which he had bound himself to accompany her image, dressed as a *penitente*, on its first outing from the Alhambra. The person was Lorca. The problem was that the rules of the Brotherhood specified that only members could take part. Moreover no free habit was available. Finally it was decided that the poet could take the place of one of the standard-bearers, men hired for the job who also wore the penitent's habit and conical, Ku-Klux-Klan-style hat.

The occasion proved a great success. The Alhambra Wood, lit by hundreds of coloured flares, took on the appearance of a sacred grove, while, high above, the bell of the Vela tolled out over the town. The following day *El Defensor de Granada* reported that the procession's progress through the wood had been 'beyond the wildest imagination'. At the end of the proceedings Lorca had disappeared as discreetly as he had come. Affixed to the cross he had carried in the procession was a note: 'May God reward you,' it said, simply. Having fulfilled his vow to the Virgin the poet returned to Madrid. No mention of his lightning visit appeared in the local press, and almost forty years were to pass before his connection with the Brotherhood of Saint Mary of the Alhambra was discovered.

We shall probably never know the motive for Lorca's participation in the procession. He was passing through a difficult period at the time, torn by conflicts and tormented by an unhappy love affair, so perhaps, like a true *granadino*, he had turned for help to the Virgin. A few months later he left for New York.

Having had a look at Santa María de la Alhambra we now enter the tiny Calle Real de la Alhambra (Royal Alhambra Street), a Mecca for all true lovers of Lorca, Falla and Granada.

Just beyond the church, on the left of the street, is the Angel Barrios Museum. It stands on the site of the famous tavern, El Polinario, run by the guitarist and flamenco singer Antonio Barrios. The building was constructed around the remains of the fourteenth-century Moorish baths in which worshippers at the Royal Mosque had carried out their ritual ablutions before prayer. If the museum is open, walk in. If it isn't, ask for the key at the Palace of Charles V.

From the end of the nineteenth century until the 1920s the house run by Antonio Barrios was one of the favourite meeting-places for Granada's artists and writers, and also attracted like-minded people passing through the town, who often left an artistic memento with the generous host. These included a fine watercolour by the American John Singer Sargent and a vellum scroll in which the Catalan painter Santiago Rusiñol (a great lover of the Alhambra) and other artists and writers named Barrios 'Consul General of Art in the Alhambra'. According to Rusiñol, Barrios possessed three qualities little found among publicans: he was an excellent flamenco singer, he understood painting and . . . he didn't mix water with his wine.

Behind the tavern there is an attractive little garden, with a pool, on the edge of the Alhambra. It was probably here that, in 1918, Lorca and three friends – Angel Barrios (son of El Polinario's proprietor), Miguel Pizarro and Manuel Angeles Ortiz – shot a 'film' invented by the poet and comprising a sequence of still photographs telling 'La historia del tesoro' ('The Story of the Treasure'). The 'film' had a straightforward plot: three Moors assassinate the guardian of a hoard of treasure. The guardian was played by Lorca. Some of the photographs have been published by Antonina Rodrigo in her book *Memoria de Granada*. The four actors had dressed up as Moors, using the facilities then *de rigueur* in the Alhambra's photographic establishments. It is the earliest record we have of Lorca's compulsive need to act out his own death – a need which greatly surprised Salvador Dalí when he met the poet in Madrid in the early 1920s:

*O tempora, O mores!* The tavern has gone, although the tiny patio where the artistic revellers gathered is still there, with its now dry basin. John B. Trend, mentioned earlier, evoked the place in his book *A Picture of Modern Spain* (1921):

One evening Sr. de Falla took me to a house just outside the Alhambra. In the *patio* the fountain had been muffled with a towel, but not altogether silenced; there was a light murmur of water running in the tank. Don Angel Barrios [ . . . ] sat there collarless and comfortable with a guitar across his knee. He had tuned it in flats so that in some odd way it harmonized with the running water, and was extemporizing with amazing resource and variety. Then his father joined us, and Sr. de Falla asked him if he could remember any old songs. The old gentleman sat there with eyes half closed, while the guitar kept up a constantly varied 'till ready', chiefly in D flat and in B flat minor, sliding down with the characteristic 'false relation' to F major. Now and again he lifted up his voice and sang one of those queer, wavering melodies of *cante flamenco*, with their strange rhythms and flourishes characteristic of Andalucía.

In September 1929 Lorca wrote to his parents from New York to tell them about his various doings and projects. 'I'm looking out of the window,' he said. 'I wish you could see this prodigious landscape of buildings and rivers with the University aristocratically in the foreground, with two magnificent granite fountains gushing out their clear water. Yes . . . but I remember El Polinario with its cypress and broken chair.'

By the time Lorca came to Granada in 1932 with the students of the touring theatre, La Barraca, Angel Barrios, who now enjoyed an international reputation as a guitarist, had taken over the tavern from his father. Here in the patio he organized a concert in honour of the youthful troupe which delighted all present.

Falla was a frequent visitor to the Barrios, who lived over the tavern. Several of his letters to father and son are displayed in the museum, as well as the originals of works by Angel Barrios, the latter's portrait by Manuel Angeles Ortiz and many other quaint and unexpected reminders of a Granada gone for ever.

On the other side of the street, opposite Santa María de la Alhambra, is a new establishment called El Polinario. It has no connection with the famous premises run by Antonio and later Angel Barrios.

In Lorca's day Calle Real de la Alhambra was one of Granada's most romantic corners, and it has preserved much of its charm. For centuries the Alhambra had its own governor and jurisdiction, and its inhabitants always considered themselves apart from the common run of *granadinos*. In the 1920s the only two entrances to the precinct, the Puerta de la Justicia and the Puerta de los Carros, were still locked at night, and to get in or out it was necessary to call the guards. Angel Barrios and Lorca were both intensely superstitious, and whenever they had to go down to the town at night through the wood they became terrified, convinced as they were that they would meet a ghost.

Manuel de Falla was in love with the deep silence that pervaded the Hill of the Alhambra at night – until, that is, things began to get noisier a few years after he arrived. Born in Cádiz in 1876, Falla had dreamt as a child of visiting the Alhambra. When, in 1907, he met Angel Barrios in Paris, his 'Granadine vocation', as one writer has called it, was encouraged. His friendship with Albéniz in the French capital further strengthened it, for, as I have said, the Catalan composer loved Granada passionately and hoped one day to return here to live.

The exact date of Falla's first visit to Granada has not been established, but it must have been in 1914 or 1915. When the composer's parents died in 1919 he felt free to begin turning his dream of living close to the Alhambra into reality. That autumn he booked in to the Pensión Alhambra, a spacious establishment, no longer extant, that ran from today's Hotel América, a few yards head of us on the left, to, approximately, the arch standing to the left of the entrance to the Parador San Francisco at the end of the street. Falla was accompanied by the painter Daniel Vázquez Díaz and his daughter. After a few weeks in the Pensión Alhambra the group moved across the street to the Villa Carmona, which was largely demolished after the Civil War to make way for excavations (part of the house still stands at No. 36). It was here, on a blustery afternoon in September 1919, that John B. Trend first met Falla. Again, I think a short quote is required (despite Trend's mistake about the elms which, as I have pointed out, were not planted by the duke):

It was the first suggestion of autumn. The tops of the Duke of Wellington's elm trees swayed in a high wind, and the pomegranate under which we were dining dropped pips in luscious, sticky envelopes on to the tablecloth. Suddenly there was a burst of rain, and every man seized his bread, plate and glass and ran for the house; I never realized the possibilities of a romantic situation so thoroughly as when I trod lightly on a rotten quince which was lying on the garden path. Sr. de Falla described the whole episode as a mixture of 'La Soirée dans Grenade' and 'Jardins sous la pluie'; but the setting was, he added, more thoroughly Spanish than Debussy could have known, for his acquaintance with Granada was derived from books and picture postcards of the Alhambra which Sr. de Falla had shown him.

The following autumn Falla returned to the Alhambra Hill. Finally, in 1921, his friends found him what he was looking for, a charming and modest *carmen* in Calle Antequeruela Alta with splendid views of the Sierra Nevada and the Vega. We will visit it in the next tour.

The Villa Carmona deserves to be remembered for another reason, for it was here, in June 1933, that Malcolm Lowry met and fell in love with Jan Gabrial. There are allusions to that journey's end in *Under the Volcano*, where we discover that the consul and Yvonne have lived unforgettable hours in Granada, and that her case, which has travelled half-way round the world, carries a Villa Carmona label. It should be added that there is no possibility that Lorca and Lowry met here that summer, since the poet was away from Granada.

The Parador San Francisco was originally a convent of the same name, built by Ferdinand and Isabella on the site of a Moorish palace of which some interesting vestiges remain. This was the first convent erected in Christian Granada, in fulfilment of a vow made by the monarchs to St Francis before taking the city. The king and queen were buried here before being moved down to the Royal Chapel in 1521, as was mentioned in Tour Two.

The Parador is one of the most delightful places in which to stay in Granada. The charming, well-kept gardens at the back border on those of the Alhambra (you can look down into the latter, which are presided over by three towers, from left to right the Torre de los Picos, the Torre del Cadí and the Torre de la Cautiva). The view of the Generalife at sundown is unforgettable from here, and from the left-hand corner of the gardens there is an unusual one of the Albaicín. In the Parador San Francisco all is peace, beauty and ease after the hurly-burly of the centre of Granada, and at night the silence is absolute.

The Parador's restaurant almost always includes on its menu, among the desserts available, some examples of local sweet-meats. If you eat here make a point of seeing which are on offer – 'huesos de santo', 'cuajadas del Albaicín', 'piononos de Santa Fe', 'tocino del cielo', they're all delicious. Remember as you try them what Lorca said about the importance of getting to know new places not only visually but also by taste and smell.

One final suggestion. Do make a point of visiting Calle Real de la Alhambra at night, when most of the tourists have abandoned the Alhambra precinct. Here it is still possible to commune with the lost Granada of Lorca and Falla. The silence is impressive, the lighting subtle, the underground water gurgles, the fountains splash in the hidden gardens, the heavy scent of jasmine is suitably oriental, the spikes of acanthus that grow in profusion along the street remind one of Greece and of Corinthian capitals . . . The place is magical, it emanates a peculiar energy.

We can now make our way back down the street to view the Alhambra, which is entered through the Palace of Charles V.

Here, in the open-air rotunda, Manuel de Falla played his *Nights in the Gardens of Spain* in 1916. The young Lorca may have been in the audience.

Lorca and his friends often wandered through the Alhambra. In those days there were far fewer tourists, and most of the time the locals had the place almost to themselves, being able to come here at night, too, when the palaces are at their most magical. The Alhambra by moonlight! Surely there can be few experiences more memorable, particularly in the spring, when the nightingales are in full song.

Disraeli, passing through Andalusia on his way to the Middle East in 1830, was deeply impressed by the Alhambra, which he termed 'the most imaginative, the most delicate and fantastic creation that sprang up on a Summer night in a fairy tale'. After lingering in these halls and patios you will probably agree. Don't miss the Sala de los Embajadores or Hall of the Ambassadors, with its fabulous star-spangled ceiling and its views across the Darro to the Albaicín. In this gorgeous setting, Ferdinand and Isabella signed the decree expelling the Jews from Spain. It was 31 March 1492.

As you wander around the Alhambra let your mind run on the role of water and reflection in the architecture of the palaces. And if you want to stand where the poet did one day, locate the Torre de las Damas (Tower of the Ladies) and its pool and, with the help of the photograph (Plate 3), situate yourself appropriately.

If you have not yet read Washington Irving's *Tales of the Alhambra*, first published in 1832, I imagine that you will want to do so as soon as possible (copies are always available in Granada). This was the book that really put the Alhambra on the map, and, despite one's apprehensions, turns out to be very readable still. Irving had lived, as Ford would do shortly after him, in the Alhambra itself – in the chambers of the Governor of the Alhambra, to be precise – and got on to familiar terms with the varied inmates of the crumbling palaces, including the ineffable Mateo Ximénez, who became his guide. Irving swam at night in the pool of the Patio of the Myrtles and was surprised to find that, in the summer, the denizens fished for swallows from the walls of the Alhambra with fly-baited hooks ('With the ingenuity of arrant idlers the ragged sons of the Alhambra have thus invented the art of angling in the sky').

Gautier, who considered the four nights he spent in the Alhambra 'the most delicious moments in my life', found a novel use for the fountain in the famous Patio de los Leones, where he and his companions had installed themselves: he set his sherry bottles to cool there.

From the gardens of the Alhambra we cross to the Generalife via a bridge over the picturesque Cuesta de los Chinos (Hill of the Pebbles), also known as the Cuesta del Rey Chico,* down which we will make our way in the next tour.

According to the etymologists, the word Generalife is Arabic for the Sublime Garden. The term is no exaggeration. The palace and gardens were created for the rest and pleasure of the Muslim kings. One could not imagine a more idyllic place to spend a holiday.

In the summer of 1924 Lorca was visited in Granada by the famous poet Juan Ramón Jiménez (later to receive the Nobel Prize for Literature) and his wife Zenobia. The hypersensitive Juan Ramón was charmed by the Alhambra and Generalife, but horrified by the outrages being committed in the town by the builders. One afternoon he said to Lorca, as the latter reported to his friend Melchor Fernández Almagro in Madrid: 'We'll go to the Generalife at five in the afternoon, which is the time when the gardens begin to suffer.' When Juan Ramón saw the celebrated Escalera de Agua (Water Staircase) he exclaimed: 'If I came here in the autumn, I'd die.'

The Escalera de Agua – follow the signposting – is certainly a marvellous work, worthy of the Muslim water-worshippers who turned this hillside into a paradise. It is so called because

---

* Boabdil, the last Moorish king of Granada, was sometimes called 'The younger', hence, in Spanish, 'Rey Chico'.

the water rushes down the scooped-out tops of the handrails that flank the staircase.

When the Venetian Ambassador to the Court of Charles V, Andrea Navagiero, came to Granada in 1526 to see the emperor, he was delighted by this contrivance. During his visit he walked in these gardens with the poet Juan Boscán, as a plaque near the staircase recalls. The meeting was to have extraordinary consequences for Spanish poetry. Navagiero, one of the great men of the Italian Renaissance, suggested to Boscán that he attempt to compose poetry, including sonnets, in the Italian manner. Boscán agreed, and his efforts were so successful that his friend Garcilaso de la Vega decided to try his hand too. If Navagiero and Boscán had not met that summer in Granada, we might never have had Garcilaso's eclogues. While there is no record of Lorca and Juan Ramón's conversations in the Generalife, they must, surely, have discussed the momentous meeting of Navagiero and Boscán that had taken place here 400 years earlier.

In the Generalife water is even more abundant than in the Alhambra. Every time I come here I remember the cry of despair emitted by the Gypsy in Lorca's 'Sleepwalking Ballad' as he climbs up to the 'high balustrades' in search of his lover, who, hypnotized by the moon, has drowned in a pool:

Dejadme subir al menos
hasta las altas barandas,
¡dejadme subir!, dejadme
hasta las verdes barandas.
Barandales de la luna
por donde retumba el agua.

Let me go up at least
To the high balustrades,
Let me go up! Up
To the green balustrades.
Balustrades of the moon
Where the water resounds.

If there's one place in Granada with 'high balustrades' and

resounding water, it's here, by the Escalera de Agua, in the heart of the Generalife.

Nearby took place, on 15 June 1919, an important event in Lorca's life. That afternoon the Arts Centre had organized a buffet in honour of Fernando de los Ríos, its ex-president, who had just been elected a Socialist MP for Granada. Present at the occasion were the famous theatre impresario and author Gregorio Martínez Sierra and his leading lady (and mistress) Catalina Bárcena. Both were much impressed by Lorca, who recited a few of his poems to the assembled company, and persuaded him to recite some more for them alone in a secluded part of the gardens. Federico acquiesced. Among the poems he chose was a composition about a wounded butterfly who falls into a meadow and is taken in by a friendly group of cockroaches, one of which, inevitably, falls in love with the ethereal creature. The latter, equally inevitably, fails to respond and, recovering the use of its wings, flies away. According to Miguel Cerón, who was present, Catalina Bárcena was in tears when the poet finished. Martínez Sierra was moved, too, promising Lorca that, if he turned the poem into a verse play, he would produce it at his theatre in Madrid, the Eslava. Thus was born *The Butterfly's Evil Spell*. Martínez Sierra was true to his word and produced the play in the Eslava on 22 March 1920, with Catalina Bárcena in the role of the love-sick cockroach. The play was a flop and it was to be seven years before Lorca succeeded in having another produced.

Lorca did not often refer directly to the Alhambra and Generalife in his work, as I have said in the introduction, but they are no less part of his sensibility for that. Having wandered here I am sure you will feel closer to the poet.

*Length: some three hours walking. The cemetery can be reached by bus or car, but the Cuesta de los Chinos (sometimes called Cuesta del Rey Chico) is only negotiable on foot.*

Leaving the Alhambra precinct by the Puerta de los Carros we set off down the hill, arriving in a few moments at a sharp loop in the road (just after the waterfall). Here, opposite a projecting wall of the Alhambra's defences (to be precise, of the Torre de las Cabezas), there is a tree-shaded bower thoughtfully provided with three stone benches and a drinking-fountain. We take the lane that leads from this down to the wood's central promenade, where we turn right. A little further on, where the path meets the asphalt main road again, is the monument to Angel Ganivet by the sculptor Juan Cristóbal.

The monument, inaugurated on 3 October 1921, has an interesting Lorca connection, recorded by José Mora Guarnido. The latter had gone one day with Lorca and the sculptor to an estate on the outskirts of Madrid, the Dehesa de la Villa, where Cristóbal wanted to make some preparatory sketches of billy goats for his Ganivet group. Several splendid specimens were on hand, and all morning, as Cristóbal drew, the friends discussed the symbolism of the goat and its place in art and poetry. Lorca was impressed by what he had seen, particularly by the animals' intense sexuality, and next morning recited to Mora and Cristóbal the poem he had just composed on the theme. 'El macho cabrío' ('The Billy Goat') was included two years later in *Book of Poems*, figuring prominently as the last composition in the collection.

A few yards beyond this spot, known as the Glorieta del Tomate, we join the main road and turn left up the hill. Ahead, to the left, tucked behind a sign-bedecked retaining wall, is a white house. Here lived the British Consul in Granada, William

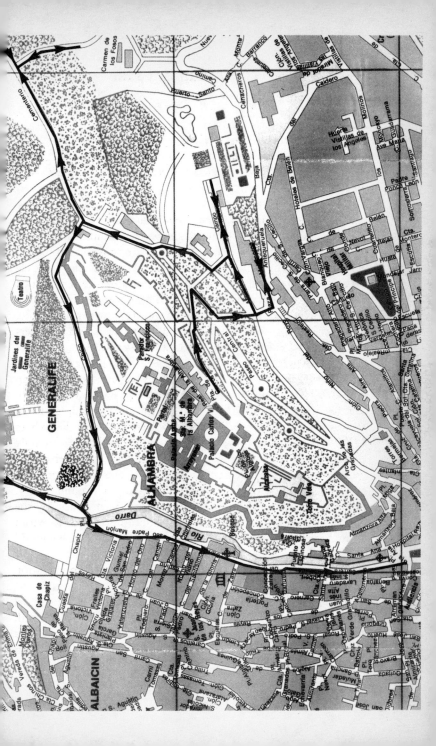

Davenhill, and his sister Maravillas. They were a charming couple, half English, half Andalusian, and, when I met them in the 1960s, constituted the last remnant of the eccentric British colony that used to live on the Alhambra Hill, which Gerald Brenan has lovingly described in *South from Granada*.

William Davenhill was a passionate mountaineer and lover of the Sierra Nevada who went down to the town as little as possible. A teller of anecdotes, he liked to recall the time he met the engineer Juan José Santa Cruz on the highest point of the Picacho de la Veleta (11,246 feet). Santa Cruz told him (this must have been in the 1920s) that he was going to build a road from Granada right to the top of the Sierra Nevada. 'For God's sake don't think of it!' the British Consul had exclaimed. 'If you build a road up here there'll be busloads of tourists, they'll build hotels, the place will be ruined! I beg you, don't do it!' But Santa Cruz was not to be put off. He built his road and today the Sierra Nevada is an international ski resort threatened by ecological devastation. Santa Cruz was one of the first victims of the Civil War, executed by the Nationalists on the vile charge of having mined the River Darro where it flows under the streets of Granada.

William Davenhill had a good story to tell too about the visit of Queen Alexandra to Granada. 'But Mr Davenhill,' she had protested on seeing the front entrance to what she thought was a small house, 'don't you think that His Majesty's Consul in Granada should inhabit more spacious premises?' Davenhill had foreseen some such comment, and as they entered the house all was clarified. The 'house' was in fact only the top floor of a suitably substantial building erected on the steep slope.

Every evening in summer the Davenhills held court on the terrace in front of the house, serving their guests an explosive cocktail made by Maravillas. There they told me about their experiences in Granada during the Civil War. The house is perched on the corner of the road leading to the cemetery, and each morning the lorries carrying victims to their execution passed this way. One morning Maravillas looked out of the window. 'It was ghastly,' she said. 'In each lorry there must have been twenty or thirty men and women piled on top of each other, trussed like pigs being taken to market. Ten minutes later we heard the shots and knew that it was all over.'

The Davenhills met Lorca once or twice, but never became friends. Really they were much more in contact with the British colony than with the *granadinos*. It seems very likely that in his ballad 'Preciosa y el aire' ('Preciosa and the Wind'), Lorca had 'Don Guillermo' in mind when he made his Gypsy girl, terrified by the wind, seek refuge in a British Consulate placed on a hilltop. True, the poem's action is set by the sea and the Consulate is 'above the pines', of which there are none in the Alhambra Wood, but the aloofness of Lorca's consul surely owes more than a little to Davenhill.

Behind the Davenhill's splendid mansion, and to their utter despair, the Duque de San Pedro Galatino built the pseudo-Moorish Hotel Alhambra Palace, inaugurated by King Alfonso XIII on 1 January 1910. The 'Palace' (pronounced 'Pala'), as it is known familiarly in Granada, cut off the breathtaking views the English had enjoyed of the Vega. Its promoter was never forgiven.

Alas, the Davenhills have gone for ever. Recently the house has been converted into flats.

We can now visit the Palace, the most famous hotel in Granada. It has played, and still plays, a vital role in the town's cultural and social life, and is rich in Lorca associations.

I suggest you go out at once on to the terrace, one of the most fabulous spots in Granada to have a drink and take in the view, particularly on a late afternoon in summer.

The terrace looks almost due south, and from here we can see clearly the havoc wrought on the Vega by the developers, who have pushed the city further and further into the plain. The new Granada could have been built towards the north, preserving the city's special relationship with the Vega, with which it used to merge almost imperceptibly, but this was not done. Each time I visit Granada and come out on to this terrace the destruction is worse. Many of us fought against the Government's and Town Council's determination to put the new six-lane bypass to the coast right alongside the city's boundary, at a stone's throw from the García Lorcas' summer house, the

Huerta de San Vicente. To no avail. Granada, today as always, persists in being its own worst enemy. Certainly Lorca and Falla would be heartbroken if they could see the view of the Vega today from the terrace of the Palace.

Let me see if I can help you to get your bearings.

Directly ahead (I am sitting at the sixth table from the left) you will see the wall of ugly blocks that is the borderline between the old and the new Granadas. Just in front of it is a squat building with a small tower. This is the Piarist Fathers College (Escolapios) mentioned in Tour One, the college which Lorca would almost certainly have attended if his father had not been somewhat anti-clerical. In front of it, invisible, is the River Genil, whose course, lined with blocks of flats, you can trace with the eye out into the Vega.

To the right of the Escolapios are the twin, grey-slated towers of the church of Las Angustias, in the Carrera del Genil.

Directly beneath us is the Church of San Cecilio, with its quaintly painted tower. This was Manuel de Falla's parish church where he came daily to pray (he was intensely Catholic).

To the right, further into town, is the cupola, with its glazed ribs, of the large Church of Santo Domingo, where Lorca's mother was baptized.

From the end of the terrace on our right we see the white *carmen* of the Rodríguez Acosta Foundation, cypress-girt and more Italian than Granadine in aspect. Beyond it, to its left, rises the massive bulk of the cathedral.

Looking now directly ahead out over the Vega, you will see at its edge an oddly shaped brown knoll with a totally bare top. It is called Montevives and has one of the largest deposits of strontium in the world. If the extractions continue at the present rate, the hill will have disappeared in a few years.

In front of Montevives and stretching away to the left is a large area of open ground, parched in summer. This is Armilla military airport, which played an important role in the Civil War.

To the left are the foothills of the Sierra Nevada which, dotted with villages, sweep up gradually to the peak of the Veleta, at the extreme left of our field of vision.

Closer to hand, almost on a level with the Veleta, we see the top of the Carmen de los Mártires and, just beyond the end of the terrace, the Manuel de Falla Auditorium. Immediately beneath the latter (be careful not to lean too far over the balcony!) is the maestro's diminutive *carmen*, with its blue-grey shutters.

Despite what the developers have done, this is still one of the finest views in Spain.

The hotel has a small theatre, in neo-Moorish style like the rest of the building. Have a look at it. On 7 June 1922, an evening of poetry and song was held here a week before the Cante Jondo Competition. Antonio Gallego Burín, member of the Rinconcillo and vice-president of the Granada Arts Centre, opened the proceedings by reading an anonymous pamphlet on 'deep song', mainly written by Manuel de Falla. Then a local flamenco guitarist, Manuel Jofré, performed. He was followed by Lorca, who recited several compositions from his *Poem of Cante Jondo*. The evening was rounded off by Andrés Segovia in the unusual role of flamenco guitarist – unusual because there is no evidence that Segovia, despite being on the jury of the contest, was particularly interested in flamenco.

The star of the concert had been Lorca, if we are to believe *El Defensor de Granada*. 'The evening was Federico García Lorca's,' it reported. 'Granada has a poet. This young lad, a dreamer in love with beauty and the sublime, is destined to become a national celebrity.'

The preparations for the great contest had put Lorca in touch with his deepest roots, and the composition of *Poem of Cante Jondo* signalled a new departure in his work. Freed from the *fin de siècle* influences which had pervaded his early poetry, he had now found his true voice – the voice that, today, everyone recognizes as uniquely his. Out of this experience would come, shortly afterwards, the *Gypsy Ballads*.

On 5 May 1929, five years after the concert in the Palace, a banquet was held in the hotel in honour of the poet and the actress Margarita Xirgu, who had just played *Mariana Pineda* in the Teatro Cervantes (see Tour One). Among those present were Manuel de Falla and Fernando de los Ríos. Salvador Dalí sent a telegram which has not, apparently, been preserved. Lorca's friend Constantino Ruiz Carnero, editor of *El Defensor de Granada*, pronounced a speech of welcome. He praised the art of Margarita Xirgu, 'our greatest actress', and called Lorca 'the most brilliant of Spain's young poets'. There was a burst of applause when he said:

García Lorca is a poet of universal horizons, but profoundly Granadine, who in a very short time has conquered the highest position in contemporary poetry. This ought to be proclaimed out loud, without fear that there may be someone ungenerous enough not to recognize it.

Moreover, we want to destroy the stupid, traditional belief that it is always people from outside who discover what is good in Granada. It was we *granadinos* who discovered García Lorca, the renovator of Spanish lyrical poetry, and it was we who told Madrid and the rest of Spain: 'We're sending you a poet born in Granada, and who expresses all the splendour of this prodigious land that is Andalusia.'

In his reply, Federico recalled the long struggle it had taken to get *Mariana Pineda* produced, two years earlier, and expressed his deep gratitude to, and admiration for, Margarita Xirgu. As for the play, although it no longer reflected his thinking on the theatre, he felt that he had done his duty 'by opposing a lively, Christian and resplendently heroic Mariana' to the cold one that stood, dressed like some free-thinking foreigner, on her pedestal. He went on to say how uneasy he felt at finding himself well known in the one part of the world, Granada, where he needed to be left severely to himself. 'It's as if they had wrenched my childhood from me,' he explained, 'and I found myself burdened with a sense of responsibility in the very place where I never want to feel responsible, where I want only to live quietly in my house, resting and preparing new work.' 'If God continues to help me and one day I become really famous,' he added, 'half the fame will belong to Granada, which made and fashioned the creature I am – a poet from birth and unable to help it.'

A few days later, on 18 May 1929, Lorca returned to the pseudo-Moorish theatre of the Palace to give an extensive recital of his work, with selections from *Book of Poems, Songs* and the *Gypsy Ballads*. The evening was a great success.

Then, in June, the poet left for New York, boarding the *Olympic* at Southampton with Fernando de los Ríos.

Leaving the Palace we turn right and begin to descend the steep hill. On our left, the Davenhills' house rises in its recently restored splendour. Twenty yards down the hill, on the left, begins the little street of Antequeruela Alta, which leads to Falla's *carmen*. The name Antequeruela (Little Antequera) alludes to the Moors of Antequera, who settled in this quarter when the Christians took that town. Falla lived in No. 11, the Carmen de Ave María, at the end of the street. He settled in in 1921, accompanied by his ever faithful sister María del Carmen, and did not leave until 1939, when he departed for Argentina, never to return to Spain.

No admirer of Falla or Lorca could fail to be moved by the Carmen de Ave María, which has been lovingly preserved almost exactly as the master left it. The upright piano; Picasso's designs for the première of *The Three-Cornered Hat* in London on 22 July 1919 at, of all places, the Alhambra Theatre; the complicated paraphernalia which Falla needed in order to roll suitably hygienic cigarettes (he was a confirmed hypochondriac); the paintings, the photographs, the spartan bedroom . . . it's all just as it was.

Lorca often played on this piano. Falla was deeply impressed by the poet's musical ability and once said: 'You know what Lorca is as a poet; well, he could have been as great or greater as a musician.' Praise indeed.

In the early hours of 1 January 1921 Lorca gave Falla a surprise on the occasion of his saint's day. The composer had retired for the night, and was aroused from his slumbers by an unholy din in the street outside. It was Lorca and a group of local musicians performing the poet's zany *ad hoc* arrangement, for trombone, horn, tuba and clarinet, of Falla's 'Canción del fuego fatuo' ('Song of the Will o' the Wisp'), from *Love the Magician*. Falla was enchanted and invited the musicians inside, asking them to repeat their feat. Lorca wrote to his friend Adolfo Salazar, the music critic, to tell him all about it. Falla, he boasted, had told him that the arrangement was splendid . . .

and that not even the great Stravinsky could have thought it up!

Don't miss the charming little garden. It and the house give a very good idea of the architecture of the typically Granadine *carmen*, which, as was explained in the introduction, derives from the Moorish concept of the inner paradise. Like Falla, the protagonist of *Doña Rosita the Spinster* lives in one of these houses, but in the Albaicín. Lorca must often have sat here with Don Manuel, and there's an interesting photograph in which he and his brother Francisco, among others, stand proudly beside Falla and the harpsichordist Wanda Landowska at the entrance (Plate 4b).

From the Carmen de Ave María, one day in August 1936, Falla set off down to the town to try and intervene on behalf of Lorca, who had been imprisoned in the Civil Government building. But it was too late: the poet had already been removed from the gaol and taken to his execution place. The intensely Catholic composer never wished to speak about what happened that day, or to name the person who, in his opinion, was responsible for the crime. All we know is that they told him that Federico was already dead.

I suggest that we now visit the nearby Carmen de los Mártires, which means retracing our steps up the hill and walking round the corner of the Davenhills' house on to the wide esplanade running alongside it. Just beyond the house, looking out over the Vega, is a great stone cross. Built in 1901 it commemorates the Christian prisoners (the 'martyrs') who died in the dungeons scattered about these parts in Moorish times.

A few paces further on we come to the entrance to the Manuel de Falla Centre and Auditorium, the work of architect José María García Paredes, the late husband of Falla's charming niece, María Isabel. It's well worth having a look inside this remarkable building, and the views from the terraces are magnificent. If you are lucky enough to be able to attend a concert during your stay in Granada, all the better.

The auditorium was erected on the site of a famous hostel, the Pensión Matamoros, run in the 1920s by an eccentric Scotswoman, Miss Laird, mentioned by Gerald Brenan in *South from*

*Granada*. The place also figures in two novels by Marguerite Steen, *Matador* (1934) and *The Tavern* (1935).

The Carmen de los Mártires, which stands amidst marvellous gardens at the end of the promenade, has been tastefully restored. During the late Franco period, with the connivance of the then Town Council, the place almost became a luxury hotel, and massive excavations were begun in the wood before the project fell through. It would have been another horror in the long list of outrages perpetrated on the landscape of Granada.

The first building occupying this site was, it seems, a hermitage erected by the Catholic Monarchs, Ferdinand and Isabella. Over it was constructed, at the end of the sixteenth century, a Discalced Carmelite convent, of which the first prior was St John of the Cross. The convent was destroyed in 1842. The present building was constructed by Carlos Calderón, a local benefactor who founded the school where Lorca's mother studied. At his death it passed to a rich Belgian, Humbert Meersmans, who died in 1934. Lorca refers to this colourful personage in his witty and ironic 'Historia de este "gallo"' ('History of this Cockerel') – an introduction to the avant-garde Granada magazine *gallo* ('*cock*') – attributing to him an inordinate passion for collecting specimens of the bird in question.

The fact that St John of the Cross had been prior of the convent (between 1582 and 1588) and wrote part of his work here deeply impressed Lorca, who greatly admired the saint's poetry. In a radio broadcast in 1936 on Granada's Holy Week he said that in Granada, one of Spain's 'nerve centres', St John's poetry, previously nourished by the stark central plains of Castile, 'fills with cedars, cinnamons and fountains' and acquires an 'oriental air'.

Retracing our steps from the Carmen de los Mártires, we turn right about 150 yards from the entrance and cut down a lane through the edge of the wood to join the main road. We turn right again and soon arrive at the Washington Irving Hotel, another survival from pre-war days.

Here, in April 1928, a young American journalist on the *New York Times*, Mildred Adams, met Lorca – and was entranced. Sitting at the hotel's battered, out-of-tune piano the poet sang his two ballads on the arrest and death of the Gypsy Antoñito el Camborio. 'In gesture, tone of voice, expression of face and body, Lorca himself was the ballad,' Mildred Adams recalled fifty years later in her book on the poet, *García Lorca: Playwright and Poet* (1977). Federico introduced the journalist to the other members of his adoring entourage, and one Sunday afternoon took her to meet Falla. She noticed that Lorca was accepted not only as a dear friend and 'disciple' of the Master, but as one of the family. Mildred Adams left Granada with copies of the magazine *gallo* under her arm, and a year later, when Federico arrived in New York, returned his hospitality.

When the war broke out in July 1936 a group of American tourists was staying on the Alhambra Hill. Among them was Robert Neville, bridge editor of the *New York Herald Tribune*. Neville, a liberal and an admirer of the Spanish Republic, kept a meticulous diary of his experiences in Granada until he was flown out to Seville on 12 August. Within two weeks he was back in New York, where, on 30 August (ten days after Lorca's assassination) he published his account of what he had seen. It made gripping reading. Neville had stayed at the Pensión América, in Calle Real de la Alhambra, and walked down each day to see his compatriots in the Washington Irving Hotel. He and they had been puzzled by the lorries that constantly trundled up to the cemetery, full of armed men. Suddenly they had understood. On 29 July he wrote in his diary:

We have solved the meaning of the outbursts of shots we hear every morning about sunrise and every evening about sunset. We have also been able to correlate it with the truckloads of soldiers that go by the Washington Irving Hotel just a few minutes before we hear those shots and which return just a few minutes after. Today four of us were playing bridge in a room on the second floor of the hotel when two truckloads went by. On the ground it would seem that all the men in those huge trucks were soldiers, but today we got a glimpse of them from above, and we saw that in the centre of each truck was a group of civilians.

The road past the Washington Irving Hotel goes to the cemetery. It doesn't go anywhere else. The trucks went up with those civilians. In five minutes we heard the shots. In five more minutes the trucks came down, and this time there were no civilians. Those soldiers were the firing squad and those civilians were on the way to execution. The men were being hauled alive to the cemetery.

On the afternoon of 30 July Neville managed to pay a brief visit to the cemetery (he does not explain how, but it was quite a feat because no civilians were allowed to approach without a special permit). That morning some Republican bombs had fallen, and the rebel authorities had announced that henceforth they would shoot five prisoners for every bomb dropped. In the cemetery Neville saw a team of gravediggers 'hard at work'.

I suggest we now follow his footsteps that afternoon.

About 200 yards further up the hill, on the left, just before the open-air terrace of La Mimbre (to which we shall return), there used to be a splendid chalet, Villa Paulina, which belonged to the historian and Anglophile Alfonso Gámir Sandoval. The building was demolished several years ago. Gámir was married to Asta Nicholson, the daughter of the writer Helen Nicholson, Baroness de Zglinitski. The latter was spending a holiday with her daughter in Villa Paulina when the Nationalist rebellion began, and described her experiences during the first month and a half of the war in her book *Death in the Morning*, published the following year in London. Referring to the early-morning Republican air-raids she writes:

On Sunday, August the second, we had our early raid at half-past four, and the second one at eight o'clock, after which we breakfasted downstairs in dressing-gowns. I remember that we were all feeling rather grumpy, for four and a half hours' sleep is an insufficient ration in war-time, when one is under a constant nervous strain. After breakfast we all dragged ourselves rather wearily upstairs, and my daughter and her husband said they were going to Mass. Not being a Catholic myself, I went to my room hoping to snatch another hour's sleep, but there seemed to be an unusual number of soldiers' lorries rattling past our house, and what with the noise they made, sounding their horns ever other minute, and the clatter from the servants' *patio*, it was difficult to doze for more than a few minutes at a time. Also I was haunted by an uneasy memory of the night before. About two o'clock I had been awakened by the sound of a lorry and several cars going up the hill towards the cemetery, and shortly afterwards I had heard a fusillade of shots, and then the same vehicles returning. Later I became all too familiar with these sounds, and learned to dread the early morning, not only because it was the enemy's favourite time for bombing us, but also on account of the executions that took place then.

During August Helen Nicholson witnessed the growing intensity of the Nationalist repression of Granada, and her own right-wing sympathies make her testimony doubly convincing.

The cemetery is about a kilometre further up the road, beyond the cluster of hotels. To the left rises the Cerro del Sol (Hill of the Sun), from whose flat top, accessible by car, there are magnificent views.

The executions took place against the cemetery walls, to the left of the entrance. How many people were liquidated during the three years of the war? At a conservative estimate it is unlikely that the number shot in Granada and the nearby villages could be less than 4,000. Over the province as a whole the total was very much higher.

In August 1936, 572 people were executed in the cemetery, according to the official burial records which I was able to consult in 1966 (they were later destroyed). No wonder Helen Nicholson was horrified.

The daily executions created serious problems for the staff of the cemetery. The bodies were thrown into common graves wherever room could be found, and eventually the cemetery had to be extended. No trace remains of these burials. After the war most of the bodies were disinterred and removed to the ossuary, a wide uncovered pit enclosed within high walls, at the western edge of the cemetery. When Brenan visited the place in 1949 the skulls of the victims, shattered by the *coup de grâce*, were pointed out to him by a helpful gravedigger. But by 1965, when I scaled the walls, the exhumed bodies of the victims had been covered by new layers of bones, shrouds and mummified skeletons.

While in the cemetery we should visit Angel Ganivet's tomb, which is situated beside the fifth cypress tree on the left of the central avenue, immediately after the entrance. Ganivet's remains were returned from Finland in 1924 and buried here, with all due honours (despite his suicide), at the end of the year. Lorca took part in the ceremony held in Madrid before the coffin was taken by rail to Granada.

Just before Ganivet's tomb, beside the third cypress from the entrance, is that of Lorca's friend, the painter Manuel Angeles Ortiz. Before he died, in Paris, he requested that his remains should be taken to the Granada which had been the main inspiration of his work.

Some 200 yards from the cemetery, as we return back down the hill, a road leads away on our left. This is the Camino Nuevo del Cementerio (New Road to the Cemetery). I suggest you walk down it a little. A clump of cypresses on the right, about 150 yards ahead, marks the spot where an eccentric Englishman, Charles Temple, ex-Lieutenant-Governor of the Nigerian Protectorate, built a crackpot house in the 1920s. Here, as Gerald Brenan records in *South from Granada*, a strangely English ceremony was enacted daily:

Every evening after tea, at the hour when the sun was getting ready to set, Mrs Temple would marshal her guests towards the veranda or, if it was cold, to the large window facing south, and pronounce in her slow, emphatic, careful voice, 'I don't think it will be long now.' We looked and waited. Gradually, the smooth, undulating summits, which up to that moment had seemed remote and unterrestrial, began to turn a pale rose, just as though a beam of a Technicolor projector had been turned on them. 'There,' she said. 'Now.' At once a silence fell upon all of us, and we sat without moving, watching the rose flush deepen and then fade away. As soon as it had completely gone everyone began talking again with the sense of relief felt by people who have just come out of church and without any allusion to what they have just witnessed.

Whether Lorca was ever present at Mrs Temple's evening rite I do not know, although we can be fairly sure that he knew about it since Brenan met at the house one evening the poet's mentor, Fernando de los Ríos, who was delighted by the so-English ceremony. Who but an Englishman would build a house on a hilltop in order to get the best view of sunset-tinged snow peaks?

In Granada today nobody remembers the Temples, and their

house is no more. This whole area was to have been developed a few years ago, turning it into an estate with villas for the rich, but the Andalusian Regional Parliament squashed the plan, thereby snubbing the Granada Town Council and, in particular, its mayor, Antonio Jara. You can see the extent to which the earth had been moved before the order prohibiting the development came through.

If you have time during your stay in Granada, I recommend that you acquaint yourself with the rest of the Camino Nuevo del Cementerio. The road loops down through the so-called Barranco del Abogado (Lawyer's Gully) between huge spiky agaves (the *pitas* of Lorca's poems), with wonderful views of the Sierra Nevada and the valley of the Genil, swings around the hill and joins the steep street just below Falla's *carmen*.

We now retrace our steps and make our way back down the hill towards the Alhambra. I suggest a halt at La Mimbre, the terrace mentioned a few pages earlier. This is one of the most delightful spots in Granada, indeed, in Spain, an ideal place for lunch when the weather allows. The food is good, the owner, Félix, and waiters are charming and witty, the surroundings, bird song (nightingales, blackcaps) and dappled sunlight a dream. As for a Lorca association, well, the *mimbre*, willow, is one of the poet's favourite trees, which gives the Lorca enthusiast a further justification for eating or having a drink here.

La Mimbre stands at the top of one of the most charming little paths in Granada – and one of the least known. This used to be called the Cuesta de los Muertos or Hill of the Dead because it was up here that the latter were carried on their way to the cemetery. Today it is known popularly as the Cuesta de los Chinos, while figuring on some maps as the Cuesta del Rey Chico (see note, p. 51). My friends in the Mimbre assure me that the name has nothing to do with the Chinese. Rather, it is an allusion to the pebbles or *chinos* which used to abound on the slope, and which were the curse of the men who earned a living by carrying the coffins up the steep hill.

Having refreshed ourselves adequately, let's make our way down the path, which has recently been widened and cleaned up and is not now quite so romantic as before. Above our heads a narrow aqueduct leads to the Torre del Agua on our left, so called because water is plentiful here (a malodorous stream used to follow the hill down to the bottom but has now been put underground). After the aqueduct we pass under the bridge we crossed on our way from the Alhambra to the Generalife in Tour Three. On the left, almost brushing the path, rise the walls of the Alhambra with the towers we saw from the gardens of the Parador San Francisco. One has the sensation of traversing a nineteenth-century print of Granada by David Roberts or Gustave Doré. Just after the last tower we come round a corner and obtain an arresting view of the Albaicín. On the right, note the low cliff full of the pebbles that give the descent its best-known name.

At the foot of the hill lived an artist who became a good friend of Lorca: the German Siegfried Bürmann, 'discovered' in Granada by Gregorio Martínez Sierra, who also, as has been related, took Lorca under his wing in 1919. Martínez Sierra engaged Bürmann to design scenery for his experimental theatre in Madrid, the Eslava. There Lorca saw him often.

The Cuesta de los Chinos leads us down to the left bank of the Darro, where it opens out into the Plaza del Aljibillo (Square of the Little Well), also known as the Plaza del Rey Chico.

If you have the energy you really should make the effort to walk upstream from here along the Darro to the Fuente del Avellano (Hazelnut Fountain), where the group of peripatetic writers captained by Angel Ganivet loved to rest and continue talking. In those days the Avellano was famous for its water, which donkeys distributed throughout the city. It's only 700 yards away.

From the road the views of the old Gypsy quarter of the Sacromonte across the river are startling: note the many empty caves, the clumps of agave (Lorca's 'petrified octupuses'), the remains of the Moorish walls leading up to the Church of San Miguel, and, to the right, the Sacromonte Abbey and its several appendages. The banks of the Darro are verdant in the extreme, and here, not surprisingly, the Muslims built villas and created beautiful gardens and orchards. The secluded spot richly deserves its name of Valparaíso, Paradise Valley.

The view from the esplanade in front of the recently restored fountain, looking back towards Granada, is marvellous, particularly at sunset.

You may like to know that above the road, but not visible from it, runs the channel that carries the water of the Darro, taken off further back up the valley, to feed the pools and fountains of the Alhambra and Generalife.

Retracing our steps we cross the Puente del Aljibillo (also called Puente del Rey Chico), the first of the thirteen bridges that used to span the Darro – only four remain – and enter the Paseo de los Tristes (The Parade of the Disconsolate), so named because it was from here that funerals used to gather before beginning the ascent of the Cuesta de los Chinos. Lorca said that Granada has 'two promenades for singing, the Salón and the Alhambra; and one for weeping, the Paseo de los Tristes, the epicentre of European Romanticism'. No doubt he had in mind the many nineteenth-century etchings of this spot, which, with its fabulous views of the Alhambra above, enthralled visiting artists.

The Paseo de los Tristes has been officially renamed Paseo del Padre Manjón, in honour of the illustrious priest Andrés Manjón, who devoted his life to educating the Gypsies of the Sacromonte and founded his first school around the corner. A small bust of Manjón presides over the *paseo*.

The Paseo de los Tristes is one of Granada's magical places in which to sit quietly with a drink and take in the scene. On summer evenings its terraces are crowded, and when the moon comes up behind the Moorish palaces the effect is so hypnotic that a hush falls on locals and tourists alike. There is nothing to equal it in Spain – except, that is, moonlight playing on the patios and pools of the Alhambra itself.

At the end of the *paseo* is the second bridge over the Darro, the Puente de las Chirimías (Bridge of the Hornpipes). Before the war it led to a picturesque terrace no longer in existence. Lorca used to go there often, and no doubt enjoyed the charming view of the Darro. In a letter to his friend the Chilean diplomat Carlos Morla Lynch he wrote: 'Sometimes I get intense attacks of tenderness which I cure drinking Granada wine in the admirable Moorish garden of Las Chirimías, where I remember you amidst the fragrant myrtles.'

The quotation gives me the excuse to mention a subject dear to my heart. Hardly any visitors to Granada realize that the province produces wine. But it does, although not in great quantity. Nowadays there are no vines in the Vega proper but they grow sparsely at Huétor, on its edge, and also, this side of the Sierra Nevada, at Pinos Genil. It's in the Alpujarras, south of the Sierra on the high slopes of the Contraviesa Mountain, that most of the vines grow. There they make what is known in Granada as 'vino de la costa', coast wine, the chief centre being the town of Albuñol, where one of the members of the Rinconcillo and a good friend of Lorca, Ramón Pérez Roda, owned a house that the poet envied because of its proximity to the sea. Richard Ford, a man who enjoyed the fine things of life, found the wine of Albuñol 'excellent'.

All these wines are amber in colour, strong and unsuitable for drinking with meals. They make an acceptable aperitif, however, and in Granada's more traditional bars and bodegas you should ask for *'un costa'* (not, NB, *'una costa'*, which means 'a coastline'). Don't waste your time trying to find the wine in the modern haunts in which the town abounds – they almost certainly won't have it. In our visit to the Albaicín I recommend two establishments that never fail (and in Tour One pointed out that Casa Enrique in the Puerta Real also stocks it).

I must add, in deference to Victor Pritchett, that his nose for good drink did not fail him in Granada, leading him to the right haunts in the Albaicín. He found the local wine 'a little like a dry port' and noted that it was 'fortifying in the heat', which, if true (I have to say I'm not convinced), sounds like another good reason for sampling it.

We return to the centre of the town down the narrow Carrera del Darro, Granada's most photographed street, which we will examine more closely in the next tour.

# TOUR FIVE The Albaicín Hill

*Length: about two hours on foot, taking one's time.*

This short but fairly strenuous tour begins in the Plaza Nueva, with its famous view of the Torre de la Vela. The square, where Cardinal Jiménez de Cisneros, Queen Isabella's confessor, burnt the 80,000 manuscript books in the Muslim University of Granada (arguing unconvincingly that they were all Korans), is dominated by the handsome façade of the Audiencia, or Law Courts, built in the sixteenth century and originally the Royal Chancellery. The prison used to be at the back of the building, and it was from here that the alleged lover of Mariana Pineda, the Liberal conspirator Fernando Alvarez de Sotomayor, escaped disguised as a Capuchin monk.

Emilia Llanos, much admired by the adolescent Lorca, lived on the second floor of the house on the corner of Calle Elvira (to our left at the edge of the square as we face the Audiencia). Here she was visited on 16 or 17 August 1936 by Federico's mother, who begged her to ask Falla to intercede on his behalf. Emilia immediately set off up the Cuesta de Gomérez, opposite, where some friends assured her that Federico had already been shot and advised her not to visit Falla. Believing that the poet was indeed dead (which he wasn't, as she discovered later), she desisted – and regretted it for the rest of her life.

On the east side of the square is the Church of Santa Ana. The entrance, in poor repair, is by Diego de Siloe, the architect of the cathedral. Inside there is a splendid wooden *artesonado*, or ceiling, but the rest of the interior is tawdry in the extreme. Lorca loved the charming tower, so obviously Moorish in inspiration. 'A tiny tower,' he described it in his 'Homage to Soto de Rojas', 'more suited for doves than bells, and made with all the style and olden-day charm of Granada.'

Beside Santa Ana – look over the wall – the Darro disappears from sight and begins its hidden course under the city. 'The

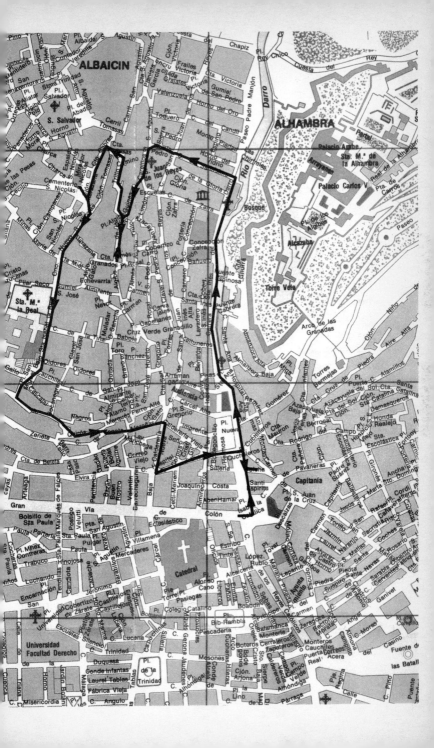

gold-bearing river moans as it loses itself in the absurd tunnel,' the young Lorca wrote weakly in his first published piece, 'Fantasía simbólica'.

The narrow Carrera del Darro, which starts here, was one of the Granada streets most favoured by the Romantic artists, who were impressed, understandably, by the view of the Alhambra Hill above. The street gives us an idea of what Calle Reyes Católicos must have looked like before the river was covered over.

The first bridge across the Darro, as we stroll up the Carrera (trying to avoid being run over by the cars) is the Puente de Cabrera. The second, some 60 yards further on, is the Puente de Espinosa. Just beyond the latter are the remains of a much larger bridge, the Puente del Cadí, which joined the Alhambra Hill to the Albaicín. As a symbol of former greatness you could not do much better than this, and the ruined bridge figures prominently in nineteenth-century prints.

Be sure to visit the delightful eleventh-century Moorish baths, the Bañuelo, just after the Puente de Espinosa, at No. 31. One of the first things the Christians did on taking over the city was to close down its numerous public baths, which they considered highly immoral. The Bañuelo is the only one still standing.

In the next street after Calle Bañuelo, Concepción de Zafra, there is a fourteenth-century Moorish house currently being converted into a museum. It has a charming patio with a pool and, if the place is open again when you visit Granada, have a look inside.

Continuing our way up the Carrera del Darro we come next to the sixteenth-century Convent of Santa Catalina de Zafra, whose nuns are famous for their traditional sweetmeats. Lorca refers to them in his lecture on Spanish cradle songs, recommending that, before visiting the Alhambra, the tourist should first familiarize himself with some of these dainties of Moorish origin, whose taste and fragrance 'give the authentic flavour of the palace when it was alive'. The *granadinos* are sweet-toothed, and Lorca was no exception. In his lecture 'How a City Sings from November to November', he returned to the theme of Granada's sweetmeats, insisting that they tell us as much about the Muslims as the convoluted tiles of the Alhambra or the horseshoe arch (which is actually of Visigothic origin). If you look through the door you will see a wooden turntable. You might try ringing the bell and asking if they have for sale any of the delicacies mentioned by the poet, such as *alfajor* or *tortas alajú*.

In his ballad 'La monja gitana' ('The Gypsy Nun'), set in an Albaicín convent, Lorca alludes to this sweetmeat-making tradition in the lines:

Cinco toronjas se endulzan
en la cercana cocina.
Las cinco llagas de Cristo
cortadas en Almería.

Five grapefruit are sweetening
In the nearby kitchen.
The five wounds of Christ
Cut in Almería.

On the other side of the Carrera, overlooking the river, is the Church of San Pedro, with the Torre de Comares in the Alhambra looming above. Just before it, on the left of the street, stands the sixteenth-century Casa de Castril. Its beautiful plateresque entrance has recently been cleaned. The building houses the Archaeological Museum, which well repays a visit. Lorca lovers will be particularly interested in the tiny bronze statuette of the goddess Minerva, found on Daimuz, the estate in the Vega which was partly owned by Lorca's father and once a Roman farm (see Tour Nine).

The museum contains numerous pieces of statuary and inscriptions from Roman Granada. The town was called Municipium Florentinum Iliberritanum, incorporated the Iberian Iliberri and was centred on the Albaicín. Not much has been possible in the way of comprehensive excavation, owing to the densely-populated nature of the quarter today. Every year new fragments come to light, however, and little by little the archaeologists are piecing together the plan of what was undoubtedly a Roman municipality of considerable importance.

Beside the Archaeological Museum is the mansion that used to belong to the powerful Pérez de Herrasti family, mentioned in *Doña Rosita the Spinster*.

Before we begin our ascent of the Albaicín, an observation on the origin of the name. According to most authorities it derives from the town of Baeza, in northern Andalusia, whose inhabitants fled to Granada before the Christian advance, settling on this hillside. The word means in Arabic, if the said experts are right, 'The Suburb of those from Baeza', just as Antequeruela, Manuel de Falla's district near the Alhambra, took its name from Antequera.

Some specialists refuse to accept this etymology, holding that the name is from the Arabic for falconer. They have convinced Laurie Lee who, in *A Rose for Winter*, has the following to say on the matter:

In the time of the Moors this high place was set aside for the breeders of falcons, who kept their hooded birds in iron cages and trained them among the rocks of the hillside. From these steep slopes one can still peer down into the city with a falcon's eye or float one's gaze across the great spaces to the mountains. The houses of the falconers still stand, white and squat, their barred windows facing the Darro gorge.

It reads well, like everything Laurie Lee writes . . . but seems to me much more the product of a lively imagination than of careful inquiry.

On Christmas Eve 1568 the *moriscos*, or forcibly converted Moors, rebelled in the Albaicín against the Christians in protest against Philip II's decree forbidding them to speak Arabic and to wear their traditional clothes. The rising was quickly and brutally crushed. Almost four centuries later the Albaicín was again the scene of repression, when, on 20 July 1936, the unarmed workers barricaded themselves inside the hilly quarter and prepared to resist the Fascists. They held out for four days before being reduced by the rebel artillery operating from the Alhambra and the main road above the quarter.

We can now begin to climb the hill. Immediately after the Archaeology Museum we cross Calle Gloria and, hugging the wall of the Convent of San Bernardo, opposite the Church of

San Pedro, arrive at the Cuesta del Santísimo. This is our departure point.

For the first 100 yards or so the going is easy. Not so once the steps begin. Before taking a deep breath, look back. A splendid view of the Alhambra is beginning to open up.

Perhaps this is a good moment to recall Lorca's vision of the Albaicín. Several pages of *Impressions and Landscapes* conjure up the narrow streets and vantage points of 'this unique and evocative quarter' in an immature prose shot through with Romantic and modernist reminiscences. Legends, superstitions, abandon, forgetfulness, the white walls of the *carmens*, the 'funereal notes' of the cypresses, the 'mysterious wells' and, above all, the absence of the people who made the quarter what it is: the Muslims. Here the poet senses 'an infinite anguish, an Oriental curse that has fallen on these streets'. In the gaze of the inhabitants of the Albaicín the young poet claims to identify a 'vagueness' which suggests that they dream of their Islamic past. Lorca must have known about the rebellion of the Albaicín *moriscos*, put down so cruelly in 1568. The Albaicín for him is a symbol of the destruction of a culture, a way of life.

Up a flight of steep steps we enter Calle San Juan de Reyes and turn right. This street, one of the most important thoroughfares in the Albaicín, is built on top of a Roman artery.

Ten yards ahead we turn left up Calle Jazmín and continue climbing. The steps at the end of the tiny cobbled street lead us into Calle Careíllo. We carry straight on, keeping always to our right (be very careful not to take the street leading down to the left). Proceeding along Calle Guinea we arrive, up a few steps to our right, at Calle Aljibe (sometimes spelt Algibe) de Trillo, which is clearly marked. You will see, behind the grille on the right, the *aljibe* (well) that gives its name to the street.

Some 300 yards further ahead on the left, after Placeta del Almez, or Almés, is the Carmen de Alonso Cano, the entrance to which comes after a large garage door. Before the war this wonderful *carmen* belonged to a great friend of Lorca, Fernando Vílchez, to whom the poet effusively dedicated one of the sections of his first book, *Impressions and Landscapes*. You might try knocking on the door to see if the owner will let you have a peep inside.

In his book *A Picture of Modern Spain*, from which I have already quoted, John B. Trend has left us an account of a memorable evening spent here in 1919. There had been a concert at the Arts Centre in honour of Falla, at which Angel Barrios and his Trio Iberia had performed. Afterwards Fernando Vílchez organized a party in the garden of his *carmen*, during which the musicians repeated part of their programme. Trend writes:

Before leaving the Carmen, our host made us follow him upstairs to another verandah, just below the roof. Here we were above the tops of the cypresses, and a vast panorama presented itself: the curved backs of the Sierra Nevada, the shadowy outline of the Alhambra Hill and its palaces, the greenish violet of the white walls bathed in moonlight with the rose-coloured blotches of the not too frequent lamps, the distant chimes, the bells to regulate irrigation, the gentle murmur of falling water. We shouted for the music of de Falla. And then, when the musicians had played till they were tired, a poet recited in a ringing voice an ode to the city of Granada. His voice rose as image succeeded image and his astonishing flow of rhetoric fell upon the stillness. What did it matter, he concluded, that the glories of the Alhambra were departed if it were possible to live again such nights as this, equal to, if not surpassing, any of the Thousand and One!

Trend explained in later versions of this chapter that the poet who performed that night was none other than Federico García Lorca.

When Lorca returned to Granada on the morning of 14 July 1936 he had with him the manuscript of *The House of Bernarda Alba*, which he had read to many people in Madrid during the preceding weeks. Shortly after his arrival he came up here to read the play to Fernando Vílchez and other friends. Within a few days the whole of Granada was to be like the 'house' ruled over by the tyrannical Bernarda. The poet had only a month to live and it is possible to see the play as prophetic.

I hope that you succeed in gaining access to this magical place. Returning the way we came we turn sharp left after the well up a steep unmarked alley that brings us into the Placeta del Comino. Here, looking over the wall of the Carmen de la

1 The building inhabited by the García Lorca family in the Acera del Casino, now demolished. They occupied the second and third floors. In the foreground, the Granadine poets José García Ladrón de Guevara and Juan de Loxa.

2 The Court of the Lions in the Alhambra. Théophile Gautier cooled his sherry in the fountain.

3 Lorca with his sisters and Zenobia Camprubí, wife of the poet Juan Ramón Jiménez, in the Patio de las Damas, Alhambra, 1924.

4a  Lorca with his brother (on the left) and two friends at the Carlos V Fountain just below the Alhambra.

4b  Lorca with Manuel de Falla, Wanda Landowska and others in the garden of the composer's *carmen*.

5a  The Huerta de San Vicente.

5b  Lorca on the terrace of the Huerta de San Vicente with his friend
the journalist Constantino Ruiz Carnero, also executed by the rebels.

6  Lorca's bedroom at the Huerta de San Vicente.

7a Víznar's little square. Falangist HQ was established in the building behind the fountain.

7b The old mill in Víznar, known as the 'Colonia', where Lorca spent his last hours. The building no longer exists.

8a The pine-clothed slopes of the *barranco* (gulley) at Víznar, where most of the executions were carried out.

8b The Fuente Grande, known to the Muslims of Granada as Ainadamar, 'The Fountain of Tears'.

Alcazaba, on our right, the view, once again, is marvellous. We keep climbing and soon see, on our right, the Carmen de Abén Humeya, a fifteenth-century restored *morisco* house. At the time of writing they serve drinks in the garden of an evening. If the house is still open during your visit, have a look inside. The view of the Alhambra is superb.

Continuing up the hill we reach some steps that take us into Callejón de las Tomasas. Straight ahead, on our left, is the Convent of the Agustinas Recoletas de Santo Tomás de Villanueva, popularly known as 'las Tomasas'. Roman remains were discovered here when the building's foundations were dug in the mid-nineteenth century. Lorca and his family loved to come to the convent chapel on Christmas Eve to attend midnight mass (in Spanish, *La Misa del Gallo*, literally Cockerel Mass), and there are several references to this predilection in his letters.

From the convent we retrace our steps along Callejón de las Tomasas. At No. 2, on our left, is one of the most delightful *carmens* in Granada, the Carmen del Alba, property of the writer José Fernández Castro. Again, you could try knocking on the door, because this is the nearest thing I know to the *carmen* in which Lorca's Doña Rosita the Spinster eats out her days as she waits in vain to hear from her distant and unfaithful lover.

There can be few houses in the world offering views to equal those obtained from an Albaicín *carmen*. In such a paradise the temptation to do nothing but contemplate is overwhelming, and it is little wonder that painters in the Albaicín find it difficult to stay at their easels. How could anyone compete with the spectacle of the Alhambra against the ever-changing backdrop of the Sierra Nevada? Capture the light, suggest the space? Try to paint anything *but* the sublime scene? Artists are said to have gone out of their minds with frustration in the Albaicín.

One of those who didn't was the Englishman George Apperley (1884–1960), from Ventnor in the Isle of Wight. Apperley fell in love with Granada and its Gypsies (one of whom he married) and settled down in the Albaicín a few years before the arrival in Granada of Manuel de Falla in 1919. Tall and thin, with a small head, he conformed almost exactly to what Spaniards expect Englishmen to look like, as did Charles Temple, mentioned in Tour Four. And just as Temple built his house on the top of the Alhambra Hill, so Apperley made sure that he had the finest position in the Albaicín.

We pass Apperley's *carmen* when, after leaving Fernández Castro's, we veer right and then turn hard left up a straight flight of steps. The Englishman's inner paradise is on our left, with a plaque ('Carmen de Apperley') over the entrance. The steps lead us to our goal, the Placeta, or Mirador, de San Nicolás, which provides an unparalleled view not only of the Alhambra but of the Sierra Nevada and all Granada. Four stone seats are provided and you will want to spend some time here to take in the beauty of the scene.

Making our way back down the steps past Apperley's *carmen* to rejoin Callejón de las Tomasas, we turn right into Camino Nuevo de San Nicolás. About 200 yards further on we reach, on our right, the entrance to the Monastery of Santa Isabel la Real.

The young author of *Impressions and Landscapes* tends to see convents and monasteries as symbols of sexual repression, and explicitly mentions Santa Isabel la Real, whose interior he had almost certainly visited while a student at the university. It was built during the sixteenth century on a site formerly occupied by a palace owned by the Muslim kings of Granada. Since the convent belongs to an enclosed order, few *granadinos* have ever been inside. The tower of the church, previously a minaret, is one of the most charming in the Albaicín, and there is a patio which may have inspired an early poem by Lorca, 'Patio húmedo' ('Damp Patio'), published in *Book of Poems*. It also seems to me very likely that the ballad 'La monja gitana' ('The Gypsy Nun'), set in an Albaicín convent, owes part of its inspiration to Santa Isabel la Real.

Fifty yards further down the street is one of the most delightful squares in Granada, the Plaza de San Miguel Bajo. The church, built on top of a mosque, contains the tombs of two distinguished seventeenth-century Granada artists: the sculptor Diego de Mora and the painter Pedro Atanasio Bocanegra. To the left of the main entrance is a thirteenth-century well where the

Muslims carried out their ritual ablutions before entering the mosque.

Along one side of the square are several establishments where excellent refreshments can be taken. The Bar Lara usually has *vino de la costa*, if you want to try it (see p. 71). In summer evenings the terraces are always crowded and this is one of the most lively spots in Granada.

At one end of San Miguel Bajo there is a tall cross. With this to our left we leave the square and proceed to the *mirador* of Cruz de Quirós immediately ahead of us. From here there is a fine view of Granada and the sunsets are gorgeous.

From the *mirador* we walk down the steep Calle Cruz de Quirós to our left. Suddenly a splendid rear view of the cathedral opens up. We turn right down some steps and sharp left into the Cuesta Marañas, which leads us down to a much wider street, Calderería Nueva. We turn right here. Calderería Nueva has become popular recently and has a selection of interesting shops and bazaars, some of them, including an exotic tea-room, run by the Muslim families who are now busily 'repopulating' the Albaicín.

Calderería Nueva leads us down to Calle Elvira. We turn left, and a few seconds later find ourselves back in the Plaza Nueva.

The Huerta de San Vicente,
the Rosales's House and the Prison

*Length: about three hours on foot.*

From the Puerta Real we set off down Calle Recogidas to visit
the Huerta de San Vicente, the García Lorcas' summer home.
The second street on the right is Calle Párraga, where Théophile
Gautier stayed. To the façade of one of the houses the Rinconcillo fixed a plaque in honour of the great man. It disappeared
when the building was demolished. A replica has recently been
installed at No. 9.

The next street is Puentezuelas, where at No. 9, on the left,
lived Lorca's great friend Francisco Soriano Lapresa, mentioned
earlier. The building, which housed Soriano's splendid library
– so generously put at the disposition of the *rinconcillistas* –
has been pulled down. It was similar to No. 7, at the time of
writing still standing but, I imagine, under death sentence with
little chance of reprieve.

On the other side of Recogidas, next to the Convent of San
Antón and on the site of the present Hotel Brasilia, stood the
Beaterio de Santa María Egipcíaca, familiarly known as 'las
Recogidas'. It was demolished in 1958. The Beaterio was founded in the sixteenth century as a refuge and penitentiary centre
for prostitutes, who were 'taken in' by the nuns (hence *recogidas*).

Here Mariana Pineda was kept under lock and key before
being escorted to prison prior to her execution. Today not a
trace of the building where Lorca set the touching last scene of
his play remains.

Mariana's house still exists, however. To see it we carry on
down Recogidas and turn into the next street, Verónica de la
Magdalena, crossing Calle del Angel and soon arriving at Calle
del Aguila. Mariana lived at No. 19 Aguila, on the left-hand
corner. Once a noble building, it is now in a state of total
abandon. A plaque affixed by the Town Council in 1870 reads:

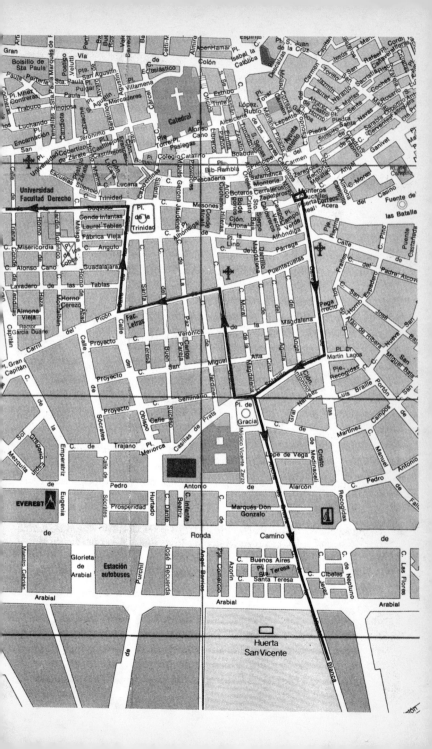

'This was the last house inhabited by the heroine Doña Mariana Pineda'.

Returning to Calle Recogidas, which retains some fine houses, such as No. 20 on the corner of Verónica de la Magdalena, we continue down the right-hand pavement and come to the next street, Solarillo de Gracia. Here, on the corner, was the Colegio de Calderón, founded at the end of the nineteenth century by the wealthy benefactor Carlos Calderón for the education of poor girls (as mentioned in Tour Four, Calderón was the owner of the Carmen de los Mártires). Vicenta Lorca Romero, Federico's mother, was one of these underprivileged children. The years she spent here turned her against convents and nuns for ever. Later, when the college no longer catered only for the indigent, her daughter Concha was a pupil. Something of the experience of both women in the school is reflected in Lorca's last, unfinished, play, *The Dreams of My Cousin Aurelia*.

Today nothing remains of the Colegio de Calderón.

On the other side of Solarillo de Gracia is the elegant if somewhat run-down mansion behind railings nicknamed the 'Casa de los Patos' ('The House with the Ducks'). The 'ducks' are the two painted swans that embellish the pond in front of the house. Until not so long ago Granada almost ended here, and began to merge with the fields and orchards of the Vega. But all that has changed.

We walk down Solarillo de Gracia, which used to be a charming street and today has lost all the grace of its name. The great seventeenth-century Cordobese poet Luis de Góngora stayed somewhere in the street during his brief visit to the city, as Lorca must have known. Soon we arrive at the Placeta de Gracia, on the other side of which, behind the trees, stands the Seminario Conciliar de San Cecilio, previously the Convent of Nuestra Señora de Gracia.

In the poet's day the Placeta de Gracia was important to the people living in the orchards and market gardens along the edge of the Vega, being a combination of social centre and 'first stop' on the way into town. Shortly after arriving in New York in June 1929, and appalled by the size and din of the gigantic city, Lorca wrote to his family to give them his impressions. They were spending the summer at the Huerta de San Vicente, which is only about 400 yards from where we are now standing. 'At the moment you're probably in the Huerta listening to the tinkle of the Seminary's bells and the distant boom of the Cathedral's,' he mused. 'As for me, I hear the sirens and rumble of New York.' Today neither the seminary's gentle tintinnabulations nor the boom of the cathedral's bells are audible from the Huerta, which has been cut off from the city by the monstrous wall of buildings that we are about to contemplate.

Before this part of Granada was destroyed by the speculators, a little lane used to lead out of the Placeta de Gracia and pick its way into the Vega. It was called Callejones de Gracia. Today its place has been taken by Ancha de Gracia and its jumble of ugly blocks.

Ancha de Gracia takes us straight down to the horror of horrors, the Camino de Ronda (bypass) built to enable north-south through traffic to avoid the centre of the town. (Today the job is done by a new motorway.) On the other side of this five-kilometre-long affirmation of Granadine philistinism rises a twelve-storey monster that says it all.

Contrive to cross the Camino de Ronda here in a break in the traffic. The mutilated Callejones de Gracia continues on the other side of the street under the name of Virgen Blanca. We continue along this and carry straight on until we cross Calle Arabial and see the walls of the Neptuno gardens and night club on our left. Twenty yards further on, on the right, is a sign-post to the Huerta de San Vicente. We traverse the car park – that's the Sierra Elvira in the distance – and make our way towards the group of cypresses and other trees which screen the house. To the right we can appreciate the extent of the tragedy inflicted on Granada by the developers.

The Huerta and its approximately 5 acres of fertile land were bought from the García Lorca family in 1984 by Granada Town Council. The house has been completely restored and, as I write, work is under way on the creation of the Federico García Lorca Park, which, apparently, is to include the largest rose garden in Europe. In other words, what was once a rural paradise on the edge of Granada, lush with running water, maize, vegetables and fruit trees, is being transformed into a conventional memorial park totally severed from the Vega by the new motorway.

Actually it's a miracle that the Huerta has survived at all (it nearly disappeared for ever during the last years of the Franco regime), so perhaps we should be grateful for small mercies.

When Lorca's father bought the place, in 1925, it was called the Huerta de los Mudos or Orchard of the Dumb. No one seems to remember why. In the sixteenth century, shortly after the fall of Granada to the Christians, it was known as the Huerta de los Marmolillos (Orchard of the Marbles). No reason for this designation seems to be have been recorded either. Before 1492 there may already have been an orchard on the site, for this whole area was once lovingly tended by the Muslims.

In honour of his wife Vicenta, Don Federico decided to rename the property and place it under the protection of San Vicente de Ferrer. An image of the saint was duly placed in a charming little *hornacina* or niche to the right of the entrance, and is still there. The choice of St Vincent was not perhaps altogether a happy one, despite Don Federico's good intentions, given the saint's appalling record as Jew-hater and enemy of heretics. When the Fascists came here looking for Lorca, there was no miraculous intervention on his part. Perhaps St Vincent did not approve of the 'Red' poet housed within these walls.

Don Federico García Rodríguez was sixty-five when he bought the Huerta de los Mudos. The idea was to have a summer home within a stone's throw of the town and, at the same time, a manageable tract of land which he could look after all year round without too much difficulty. There was no question, that is, of abandoning the family flat in the Acera del Casino.

From 1925 onwards summer in Granada would be inseparable in Lorca's mind from the Huerta de San Vicente. Here with his parents, surrounded by adoring sisters, uncles, aunts and cousins, the cock of the roost, Lorca was always able to work happily and productively. And, when absent from Granada, the peace, water and luxuriant vegetation of the little paradise were never far from his thoughts. 'I'm now at the Huerta de San Vicente,' he wrote to the poet Jorge Guillén in 1926. 'There's so much jasmine and nightshade in the garden that we all wake up with lyrical headaches.'

After looking at the living room downstairs, where Federico had his piano, go up to his bedroom, which contains the table he worked at, one of the original 'La Barraca' posters, designed by Benjamín Palencia, his bed and a painting of the Virgin of Sorrows by Rafael Alberti done for the poet in 1924 to celebrate their meeting at the Residencia de Estudiantes in Madrid. The dedication reads: 'To Federico García Lorca this view of the South to mark the inauguration of our friendship.'

From his balcony Lorca loved to gaze across the Vega to the snow-covered peaks of the Sierra Nevada. He could also see the Alhambra and Generalife, today cut off by the buildings along the Camino de Ronda. 'I'm in the Huerta de San Vicente, a paradise of trees and clear water,' he wrote to his friend Melchor Fernández Almagro in the summer of 1928, just after the publication of the *Gypsy Ballads*. 'Granada is stretched out in the distance opposite my window, more beautiful than ever.'

That Granada is no longer visible. Luckily, however, the speculators have not been able to suppress the splendid view of the Sierra Nevada and from here the Picacho de la Veleta can be seen in all its majesty. 'Today it's a grey, grey day in Granada,' Lorca wrote in September 1928 to another friend, Jorge Zalamea. 'From the Huerta de San Vicente (my mother's called Vicenta), where I live among magificent fig-trees and robust walnuts, I have the best mountain view (through the air) in Europe.'

The poet had arrived back in Granada that summer in a deep depression not unrelated, probably, to his frustrated love life. In the same letter to Zalamea he complained bitterly: 'You can't imagine what it's like for me to spend night after night at my open window looking out over a nocturnal Granada that is *empty* for me and without consolation of any kind.'

This window (*balcón*) is surely the one alluded to in the poem 'Despedida' ('Farewell'), included in *Songs*:

Si muero
dejad el balcón abierto.

El niño come naranjas.
(Desde mi balcón lo veo.)

El segador siega el trigo.
(Desde mi balcón lo siento.)

¡Si muero,
dejad el balcón abierto!

If I die,
Leave the window open.

The child's eating oranges.
(From my window I can see him.)

The reaper's reaping the corn.
(From my window I can hear him.)

If I die, please
Leave the window open!

At this desk Lorca worked on the *Gypsy Ballads*, *Songs*, *The Public* (begun in La Havana and finished here), *When Five Years Pass*, *Blood Wedding* and *Doña Rosita the Spinster*, aided by records played on the gramophone that is still part of the house's furniture.

In the summers of 1934 and 1935 Lorca was visited here by his friend the Galician writer Eduardo Blanco-Amor, who took various photographs of the poet in the Huerta.

From the poet's bedroom go on to the first-floor terrace, from which there used to be a good view of the Alhambra and Generalife. Lorca loved to come out here, and there is an excellent photograph (Plate 5B) of him standing by the balustrade with his friend Constantino Ruiz Carnero, the editor of *El Defensor de Granada*, also assassinated at the beginning of the Civil War.

In front of the house, beside the lane, are two cypresses. They were planted by Federico and his brother Francisco.

Lorca returned to the Huerta de San Vicente for the last time on the morning of 14 July 1936, terrified by the atmosphere of growing violence in Madrid, where the ultra-right-wing MP José Calvo Sotelo had just been murdered.

On his arrival he was delighted to find that a telephone had recently been installed in the Huerta, and probably called Constantino Ruiz Carnero at *El Defensor* to tell him he was in town. The following day's issue of the paper announced prominently, in the centre of its front page, that Lorca had returned to Granada to spend 'a brief period' with his family. Lorca's presence was also noted by the town's other two leading newspapers. The conspirators must have become aware immediately, that is, that the poet was among them. Moreover Lorca, never one to stay indoors, was seen in the town during the six days leading up to the rising against the Republic, which began in Granada on 20 July.

Every 18 July, St Frederick's Day, the García Lorcas held open house at the Huerta in honour of the father and eldest son, both Federicos. Relatives and friends would arrive, bearing gifts, from Granada and the villages of the Vega, and the revelry would continue until well into the night. But that year things were different. The previous evening the feared anti-Republican revolt had broken out in Spanish Morocco, and in the morning it became known that General Franco, commander of the Canary Islands, had thrown in his lot with the rebels. Things were looking very serious indeed, despite the Government's assurances that the rebellion was under control. On the evening of 18 July there was great confusion in Granada, and panic when rumours that General Queipo de Llano had taken Seville began to spread. That the rumours were true was confirmed the following morning.

What happened in Granada during the next few days can be résuméd briefly. General Campíns, the Military Governor, had only been in command for a week. A loyal Republican, he appears to have had absolute confidence in his officers, who assured him that they were not involved in any plot. When he found out what was really happening it was too late – far too late. As for César Torres Martínez, the Civil Governor, he, too, had only just arrived in Granada and knew hardly anyone. He obeyed the Government's orders not to distribute arms to the masses, thereby contributing, in good faith, to the easy triumph of the rebels when the garrison and the Fascists took to the streets on 20 July.

The only resistance was in the Albaicín, as was said earlier. There the Republicans, almost without guns, held out for four days before being crushed.

When it became obvious that the *coup d'état* had failed and was now turning into full-blooded civil war, the rebels decided to impose a reign of terror in Granada to intimidate the citizens and make it more difficult for the Government to recover the city, which was practically surrounded by Republican territory. Thus began one of the blackest periods in the entire history of Granada.

Here in the Huerta de San Vicente the family were desperately worried about Manuel Fernández-Montesinos, Concha García Lorca's husband and Socialist Mayor of Granada, who was among the first people arrested on 20 July. According to one neighbour, Federico visited Montesinos in gaol shortly after his arrest and returned to the Huerta violently ill, taking to his bed. What he had seen had terrified him.

One of Lorca's close friends in Granada, Eduardo Rodríguez Valdivieso, visited him several times after the war began. One afternoon the poet came out of the house pale and trembling. He had been having a siesta upstairs in his bedroom, he told him, and had had a terrible dream in which he was lying on his back on the ground surrounded by a group of mourning women dressed from top to toe in black. Each of them had menaced him with a black crucifix. The poet felt sure it was an evil omen.

He was proved right. On 6 August, a Falangist squad arrived at the Huerta and searched the premises. Looking for what? There was a rumour at this time, no doubt put about by Federico's enemies, that he had a clandestine radio in the house with which he was in touch, of all things, with *the Russians*. Perhaps the group was searching for the improbable transmitter. They found nothing and left.

The following day Alfredo Rodríguez Orgaz, a young friend of the family who until recently had been City Architect of Granada, appeared at the Huerta. He had been hiding since the beginning of the rising and, realizing that he was in extreme danger, had now decided that he must escape. Federico's father assured him that that night some peasant friends of his would take him across country to the Republican zone, only a few kilometres away. Federico told Rodríguez that he had been listening to the Madrid radio, with its regular Government bulletins, and was convinced that the 'war' would be over in no time. There could therefore be no question of his accompanying him. Just then someone gave the alarm. A car was approaching down the lane. Perhaps they were after Rodríguez Orgaz! Alfredo bid a hasty farewell and dashed behind the house, where he hid under some bushes. The unwelcome visitors were indeed looking for the architect. But on finding no trace of him they left. That night Rodríguez reached Santa Fe – and safety.

Then, on 9 August, things took a decided turn for the worse, when another group of Fascist thugs arrived at the Huerta, looking this time for the brothers of the caretaker, Gabriel Perea, who lived in the house alongside with his mother and sister. The brothers were wrongly accused of having killed two men in the village of Asquerosa (Lorca's 'second' village in the Vega, which we shall be visiting in Tour Nine), and the Fascists thought that Gabriel might know of their whereabouts. Most of the men were from Pinos Puente, just down the road from Asquerosa, and among them were the landowners Miguel and Horacio Roldán Quesada, enemies of Federico's father and known for their ultra-conservatism. The group searched Perea's house, and then proceeded to pitch his mother down the stairs. Where were her other sons, the assassins? When the poor woman insisted that she did not know, they hauled her and the rest of the family out on to the terrace in front of the Huerta. There they tied the terrified Gabriel to a cherry tree and one of them began to beat him with a whip. The poet, who was witnessing this scene with his parents and sister Concha, could stand it no longer and rushed forward to protest Gabriel's innocence. He was thrown to the ground and brutally kicked. The group knew exactly who he was and one of the men snarled, 'Ah, the little queer friend of Fernando de los Ríos!' Lorca retorted that he was a friend not only of the famous Socialist professor, but of many people of different persuasions. It seems that, before taking Gabriel away for interrogation in the Civil Government building (he was released later that evening and returned to the Huerta badly shaken), they warned Lorca that he was under house arrest and must on no account leave the premises.

While these scenes were taking place, Angelina Cordobilla, Concha García Lorca's maid, managed to hurry the latter's three children out of the house and take them to the *huerta* immediately behind, which belonged to a close friend of the family, Francisco Santugini López.

(The modest building was expropriated in 1990 and razed to the ground. Surely it should have been respected and given some new use – say, to house the instruments necessary for the maintenance of the park? But no, no one thought of that, no one remembered Angelina Cordobilla's exploit or the close friendship uniting the García Lorcas and the Santugini Lópezs. The place had to be cleaned up to make way for, perhaps, another bed of roses, and in a few minutes a bulldozer reduced so much history and beauty to a heap of rubble.)

The poet was now frightened. The next time they might well come for him. He must get away from the Huerta. But to where? To whom could he turn for protection? Then he thought of his friend the young poet Luis Rosales, who had returned to Granada, like himself, just before the rising began. Two of Luis's brothers, José and Antonio, were leading Granada Falangists. And was it not a fact that Luis, twelve years younger than Federico, considered him his poetic *maestro*? Lorca had seen a lot of Rosales recently in Madrid and their friendship had grown stronger. Of course Luis would help! Federico immediately telephoned the Rosales's house, and was fortunate in being able to contact his friend straight away. Rosales arrived shortly afterwards at the Huerta, accompanied by his younger brother Gerardo.

Luis Rosales has described many times what was said at the ensuing family discussion. There were basically three possibilities: to drive Federico to the Republican zone, which would have been easy for Rosales to arrange; to install him in Manuel de Falla's *carmen*, which Rosales was convinced no one would dare violate; or for Luis to take him to his parents' house, which, given the Falangist status of the Rosales, was surely completely safe. Lorca opted for the third possibility.

Before Rosales left the Huerta he told the family not to reveal Lorca's whereabouts. That night the poet was driven to the Rosales's house in the centre of Granada in the taxi owned by Don Federico's driver, Francisco Murillo.

We will follow the probable route they took shortly, but first, once you feel ready to leave the Huerta, I propose that we visit the nearby Huerta del Tamarit (off our map), also important in Lorca's life.

To do so, we turn right after crossing the car park and make our way down Virgen Blanca. The road, in Lorca's day a mere cart track, used to lead to a miniature bridge over the irrigation channel known as the Acequia Gorda (Big Watercourse), built by the Arabs, and then continued out into the Vega under the name of Callejón de los Nogales (Walnut Lane). But, in 1990, the Acequia Gorda was rerouted and the bridge knocked down to make way for the roundabout at which we now arrive. If Lorca saw the scene today he would die of anguish.

Crossing under the flyover we will find the continuation of the Callejón de los Nogales (not signposted as such) on the other side of the roundabout, exactly opposite Virgen Blanca and immediately before the slip road leading up on to the motor-way (direction Motril).

The Huerta del Tamarit is about ten minutes' walk away, on the left among the fields. A narrow, tree-lined avenue leads to it.

The Huerta del Tamarit belonged to Lorca's uncle, Francisco García Rodríguez, whose daughter Clotilde was one of the poet's favourite cousins. When he bought it there was only one house. He then built another alongside, which is the first you will see. Lorca often came here and loved the place. He once said that his uncle had the most attractive address in the world: 'Huerta del Tamarit, Término de Fargüi, Granada.' The poet must have appreciated the Arabic ring to this – Fargüi was the name given to the district by the Muslims, and Tamarit comes from the Arabic for date palm. Lorca used to claim that the Huerta del Tamarit was even more beautiful than the Huerta de San Vicente. 'Clotilde,' he once said to his cousin, 'your *huerta* is a collection of picture postcards.'

The Huerta del Tamarit is still beautiful, indeed almost as it was in 1936, and has a lived-in quality absolutely lacking now in the Huerta de San Vicente. Lorca immortalized it in the title of his *Diwan of the Tamarit*, a collection of poems in honour of the Islamic poets of Granada. One of these, 'Casida de los ramos' ('Qasida of the Branches'), has been felt by some readers to contain a premonition of Lorca's assassination, for we know that when the poet fled from the Huerta de San Vicente his enemies came to the Tamarit looking for him:

Por las arboledas del Tamarit
han venido los perros de plomo
a esperar que se caigan los ramos,
a esperar que se quiebren ellos solos . . .

Through the groves of the Tamarit
Have come the dogs of lead
To wait for the branches to fall,
To wait for them to crack unaided . . .

Walking back now through the destroyed landscape to the Camino de Ronda, we retrace our steps to the Placeta de Gracia. When Francisco Murillo drove Lorca from the Huerta de San Vicente to the Rosales's house, it seems likely that he would have come this way, although we cannot be sure.

Two streets lead out of the square in the direction of the centre of town, Moral de la Magdalena and Gracia. We can take either of these, crossing two streets (San Miguel Alto and Verónica de la Magdalena) and, arriving in Puentezuelas, turning left. At the end of the street is the building that used to house the Faculty of Philosophy and Letters of Granada University and which today is the University School of Translators and Interpreters. Turning right we are now in Calle de las Tablas. The third street on the left is Angulo, Lorca's destination. The Rosales lived at No.1 in a spacious house on the corner of Tablas. The site is now occupied by the Hotel Reina Cristina.

The interior of the fine house has been altered almost beyond recognition. It was of typical Granadine design, comprising an entrance hall with numerous rooms built around an ample patio, where the family lived in summer, and, upstairs, two floors and a rooftop terrace. On the second floor, in what was virtually an independent flat, lived Mrs Rosales's sister, Aunt Luisa Camacho. It was decided by common consent to install the poet with her.

The patio is now the hotel's dining room. The elegant columns have gone, as has the broad staircase that led up to the first floor. But the owners have retained the door through which Lorca's enemies pushed their way on the afternoon of 16 August 1936. Anyone who wants a clear idea of what the house was like before the war should read Luis Rosales's book of memoirs, *El contenido del corazón* (1969).

In one of the rooms off the patio Luis Rosales had his library, and we know that during the eight days Lorca spent here he made good use of it.

Whenever a Republican plane appeared over Granada, Lorca and the women of the house – Mrs Rosales, her daughter Esperanza, Aunt Luisa Camacho and a servant – would rush downstairs to hide in an improvised air-raid shelter the poet nicknamed 'El Bombario'.

Little by little, thanks to the attentions of the women, Lorca seems to have regained a modicum of tranquillity, telling them about his experiences in New York, Buenos Aires and Cuba and playing folk songs on the piano which the familiy moved specially into his room. As for the Rosales menfolk, Lorca scarcely saw them: the father was busy most of the time with his shop off the Plaza de Bib-rambla (we saw the site in Tour Two); Miguel and José were married and had their own flats; and Gerardo, Luis and Antonio hardly slept at home at this time.

Lorca could not possibly work under such conditions. Every day he perused the local paper *Ideal*, which gave a very slanted version indeed of what was happening in and outside Granada. Above all, he listened to the radio, both the Nationalist and the Republican, joking with Esperanza about the incredible versions of events being given by both sides. As for his projects, he spoke enthusiastically about the book of sonnets he was going to publish, and claimed that soon he was going to get down to an epic entitled *Adam*, along the lines of *Paradise Lost*, which he had been thinking about for several years.

How much can the poet have known about the ruthless repression then taking place all around him? While he cannot have been aware of the full horror of what was happening, it is impossible to doubt that he knew about the executions in the cemetery, for these were sometimes mentioned prominently – and approvingly – in *Ideal*. He must have been deeply worried about the fate of his brother-in-law too, since random executions were being carried out in alleged reprisal for the feeble Republican bombings of the town. It seems unlikely that he would not have asked the Rosales brothers to intervene on Manuel's behalf.

According to Esperanza Rosales, Lorca occasionally talked to his family by telephone. But of these conversations, doubtless very brief and to the point, given the danger of being overheard, no record remains.

The poet's time was running out. Shortly before sunrise on 16 August 1936 – it was a Sunday – Manuel Fernández-Montesinos was shot in the cemetery along with twenty-nine other victims. The terrible news immediately reached Lorca, who was shattered. Moreover he probably knew that his enemies were on his track, for the previous day another group had gone to the Huerta looking for him. On discovering that Lorca was no longer there, they had combed the house and even dismantled the baby grand piano in search of incriminating papers – or perhaps the phantom radio. The leader of the group had threatened Concha that if she didn't tell them where the poet was, they would take her father away instead. Terrifed, Concha had blurted out that Federico was staying with a Falangist friend of his in Granada, another poet. Perhaps she had even given Rosales's name.

The person who arrived at the Rosales's house to detain Lorca was Ramón Ruiz Alonso, an ex-Member of Parliament who belonged to the right-wing Catholic coalition party led by José María Gil Robles. Ruiz Alonso had taken an active part in the plot against the Republic, and seems to have had a personal grudge against both Lorca and the Rosales.

None of the Rosales menfolk was at home when Ruiz Alonso arrived at Calle Angulo No. 1 accompanied by two henchmen and a sizeable armed contingent that cordoned off the street in a large-scale operation mounted on the orders of the new Civil Governor, Valdés. Mrs Rosales stood up bravely to Ruiz Alonso and refused point-blank to allow him to take the poet away. How dare he come to a Falangist house on such a mission? Why did they want to question Lorca? According to Esperanza Rosales, Ruiz Alonso replied that the poet was in trouble because of what he had written.

Mrs Rosales tried to locate her sons by telephone, and was eventually able to speak to Miguel at Falange HQ in the nearby Calle San Jerónimo. It was agreed that Ruiz Alonso should drive there immediately to consult with him about what was to be done. Soon afterwards the ex-MP returned with Miguel. Rosales was amazed to find the street full of armed men.

Miguel explained to his mother that, in the circumstances, he had no option but to allow Ruiz Alonso to take Federico to the Civil Government building. He would accompany them person-ally to find out what the problem was. Esperanza then went to fetch Lorca, who must have been listening to the proceedings from an inner window upstairs. On top of the piano there was an image of the Sacred Heart of Jesus to which Aunt Luisa Camacho was devoted. Before Federico went downstairs the three of them prayed in front of it, at Aunt Luisa's prompting.

In 1956 Luis Rosales told the Spanish-born American researcher Agustín Penón that Lorca was now in a state of almost complete collapse, trembling and weeping. Luis must have learnt this when he returned home that evening. As he took his leave of the women, the poet murmured to Esperanza, whom he had nicknamed his 'Divine Gaoler', 'I'm not going to shake hands with you, because I don't want to think we're never going to meet again.' She never forgot that sentence.

Then, with Miguel Rosales and Ruiz Alonso, he went out into the street, through the door that has been preserved in what today is the dining room of the hotel.

Opposite the Rosales's house lived the owner of Los Pirineos, a bar on the corner of the nearby Plaza de la Trinidad. (Don't bother looking for it – it no longer exists.) One of the sons, then twelve years old, who had been told by the armed men to get indoors, peeped through the window and saw the poet step out from the doorway of No. 1 Angulo. He was wearing dark grey trousers and a white shirt with a loose tie, and had his jacket over his arm. The group walked to the end of the street and round the corner into the Plaza de la Trinidad where, it seems, the men had parked the car waiting to drive Lorca the short distance to the Civil Government building.

The car almost certainly turned sharp left out of the plaza up Calle Duquesa, the fourth street after Angulo.

During the brief journey, according to Miguel Rosales, the poet begged him to intervene at once on his behalf with the authorities and, above all, to get hold of his brother José, one of the most important Falangists in Granada. José would soon sort the matter out.

Let's follow them up Duquesa. In a few moments the street intersects with Calle Málaga. Opposite, on the corner, is the Botanical Garden, which belongs to the university. We cross the street and continue up Duquesa. On our left is the Jefatura Superior Policía. The same building was Police HQ in 1936. A few yards further on, on the right, we arrive at the back door to the Faculty of Law. When the war began, this was the *front* entrance to the Civil Government building (which returned to Granada University in 1944). The door is normally shut.

It was here that the most crucial incident in the rising took place when, towards six in the afternoon of 20 July 1936, a detachment of soldiers from the Artillery barracks and a group of Falangists led by Valdés managed to persuade the guards defending the building to throw down their arms. The Civil Governor, César Torres Martínez, was arrested in his office along with other political leaders. Not a shot was fired. Meanwhile other vital centres in Granada were occupied by the rebels.

Lorca was driven to this spot on the afternoon of 16 August 1936 and hustled up the steps that then led to the entrance.

To get inside the building, unless you're in luck and the door happens to be open, take the first turn right (Calle Colegios) and walk around the block to the main entrance of the Law Faculty in the corner of the Plaza de la Universidad, mentioned in Tour Two. Once through the door turn hard right down the passageway leading to a patio with cypresses and a dry fountain. If you cross this diagonally you will find yourself in a space that opens on to what was the patio of the Civil Government building, on the other side of which are steps leading down to the back door that we saw from Calle Duquesa.

Despite the many modifications to the building that have been effected since 1944, it is not difficult, I think, to evoke the scenes that took place here throughout the war, with their quota of brutality and human misery. Lorca spent two nights, perhaps three, in the building, somewhere upstairs. He was seen there at least once by his sister's maid, Angelina Cordobilla, who brought him food, cigarettes and clean linen. Others who saw the poet then have stated that he was in total despair and in pain from the bruises resulting from the incident in the Huerta when he intervened on behalf of the caretaker, Gabriel Perea.

When Miguel Rosales left Lorca here in the crowded patio he hurried back to Falange HQ and tried desperately to contact his brother José by telephone. To no avail. Nor could Miguel locate Luis or Antonio, both of whom were at the front.

When Luis and José arrived back in Granada that evening they were outraged to learn what had happened. They decided to confront the Civil Governor immediately, and hurried here with some other Falangist friends, including one Cecilio Cirre. They were informed that Valdés had not yet returned from a visit to Lanjarón, in the Alpujarras. In 1966 Luis Rosales told me what happened next:

There must have been a hundred people in the room. It was packed. Among them was Ramón Ruiz Alonso, whom I didn't know by sight. I knew no one there. I said, with violent hatred: 'Who is this Ruiz Alonso who went to our house to remove without either a written or a verbal warrant someone staying under the roof of his superiors?' I stressed the 'this Ruiz Alonso', and repeated the question a couple of times. Then – I was speaking with passion, with hatred in my voice – one of the individuals present stepped forward. 'I am *this* Ruiz Alonso,'

99

he announced. I asked him before the whole gathering (there were a hundred people there who could confirm the accuracy of this) how he had dared go to my house without a warrant and arrest my guest. He replied that he had acted on his own initiative. I said to him: 'You don't know what you're saying, repeat it!' I was fully aware of the poignancy of the moment and wanted to be sure that both I and those present remembered the exact words spoken. So I repeated the question three times and each time he replied: 'I acted on my own initiative.' Then I said to him: 'Salute and get out!' 'Who, *me?*' he replied. Cecilio Cirre was great, and got hold of Ruiz Alonso and said to him: 'You're speaking to a superior! Now salute and get out!' Finally, since nobody stood up for him, Ruiz Alonso left.

Confronted with this tape-recorded testimony in 1966, Ruiz Alonso denied that he was present during the scene described by Rosales, alleging that, after leaving Lorca in the Civil Government building, he returned home. None the less the evidence (not all of which, obviously, I can repeat now) is overwhelmingly in favour of Rosales's account.

Later that night José Rosales returned here to confront Valdés. There was a violent discussion. According to a statement made by Rosales shortly before his death in 1978, the Civil Governor had on his desk a typewritten accusation against the poet, drawn up and signed by Ruiz Alonso. It stated that Lorca, a subversive writer, had a clandestine radio at the Huerta de San Vicente with which he was in contact with the Russians; that he was a homosexual; that he had been the secretary of Fernando de los Ríos (which was not true); and that, moreover, the Rosales brothers were betraying the rebellion by sheltering a notorious Red.

Did a confrontation take place between Lorca and Valdés before the fatal order was given? It is impossible to say. Valdés carried his secrets with him to the tomb on 5 March 1939, a victim of cancer and of a wound received in action after he was removed from his post in Granada in 1937.

Lorca left the building handcuffed to another prisoner, a primary school teacher from Valladolid called Dióscoro Galindo González. Accused of being a Communist, he had been arrested at his home in a village outside Granada by a group of Falang-ists.

A young friend of Lorca, Ricardo Rodríguez Jiménez, hap-pened to see him and Galindo González being taken out. Rodríg-uez had an atrophied right hand and, several years earlier, Feder-ico, aware of the boy's musical ability, had bought him a specially made small violin. It was a gesture typical of the poet. Rodríguez had been playing cards with a friend in Police HQ across the street from the Civil Government building in Calle Duquesa. He left the station after the last bulletin on Seville Radio, around 3.15 a.m., and suddenly heard someone call his name. It was Federico, whom Rodríguez was aghast to see handcuffed to an older man and surrounded by members of the 'Black Squad', men who had been given *carte blanche* by Valdés to assassinate and torture, and who enjoyed the work. 'Someone stuck a gun in my chest,' recalled Rodríguez in 1980. 'I screamed "Murderers! You're going to kill a genius! A genius! Mur-derers!" I was arrested and taken into the Civil Government building. They locked me up for two hours and then let me out.'

A few seconds after this incident the killers pushed Lorca and Galindo González into the car waiting to drive them to their place of execution in the hills outside Granada. We shall follow the route they took in Tour Eight.

## TOUR SEVEN The Sacromonte and the Church of San Miguel el Alto

*Length: about three hours on foot. If you're in a hurry, or lack sufficient energy, you can drive up to both the Sacromonte and the Church of St Michael, but it's not such fun (see note at the end of the tour). I recommend that you take a copy of the* Gypsy Ballads *with you so as to be able to read Lorca's ballad 'San Miguel' on the spot.*

*A word of warning: tourists are sometimes harassed in the old Gypsy quarter, and there have been muggings along the last, lonely stretch of the way up to the Church of St Michael, so watch yourself and, if you're a woman, perhaps it would be wise to be accompanied.*

This tour begins in the Paseo de los Tristes (officially called the Paseo Padre Manjón) at the end of the Carrera del Darro, where we start off up the Cuesta del Chapiz, the main access to the Albaicín. When the garrison against the Republic rose on 20 July 1936, the workers cut a deep trench across the bottom of the street to prevent vehicles from climbing the steep hill. It did them little good.

At No. 4 Cuesta del Chapiz, on the right, is the Casa de los Córdova, which houses the City Archive. On the left is the Escuela de Ave María, one of the schools founded by Andrés Manjón for the education of poor children and Gypsies. It is this worthy's name that has been given to the Paseo de los Tristes.

A hundred yards further up, on our right, is a Moorish palace known as the Casa del Chapiz, seat of the School of Arab Studies, founded by the Republic in 1933. If it is open, have a look inside. It would be hard to imagine a more delightful spot in which to study the Muslim civilization of Granada.

We now take the road to the Sacromonte, which begins immediately after the Casa del Chapiz on our right. This used to be the main road to Guadix, and is superimposed on the

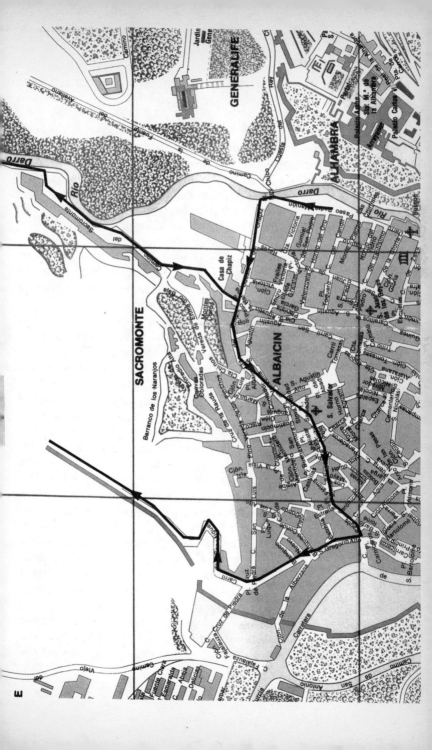

thoroughfare that linked Roman Granada – the Municipium Florentinum Iliberritanum – to that town (then called Acci). We soon come on our left to the celebrated Gypsy quarter of Granada, today very much declined. In 1962, after torrential rains, many of the caves collapsed and the authorities decided to move most of the families to another, more modern, part of Granada, with the results that can be imagined. None the less, there are still some Gypsy families living here and one or two caves continue to stage Gypsy *zambras*, the wild dances that so delighted the nineteenth-century tourists.

Among the latter was the Russian composer Glinka, who spent several months in Granada during the winter of 1845. He struck up a friendship with a well-known local flamenco guitarist, Francisco Rodríguez Murciano, who introduced him to the *cante jondo* of the Sacromonte's Gypsies. Glinka, fascinated by the possibilities for his own work afforded by Spanish folk music, began the experiments that led to his *Jota aragonesa* (1845) and *Summer Night in Madrid* (1848), which in turn sparked off both a new interest in folk song in Russia and a spate of Spanish-inspired pieces by foreign and national composers. Falla was interested in Glinka, and passed on his enthusiasm to Lorca. In his lecture on *cante jondo* in 1922, the poet talked about the consequences of Glinka's visit to Granada, concluding: 'And so you see how the sad modulations and grave orientalism of our *cante* were imparted by Granada to Moscow, and how the melancholy of the Vela bell is echoed by the mysterious bells of the Kremlin.'

The Sacromonte, with its caves, prickly pears (*chumberas*), agaves (*pitas*) and denuded slopes crowned by the Church of St Michael the High, is the setting that inspired the landscape of many of the poems in *Poem of Cante Jondo* and *Gypsy Ballads*. It seems likely, for example, that in the 'Ballad of the Moon, Moon' Lorca was thinking of some Gypsy forge he had seen hereabouts, while the dark hill down which Soledad Montoya comes in 'Romance de la pena negra' ('Ballad of Black Anguish') is surely an allusion to this 'Holy Mountain'. As for the 'Ballad of the Spanish Civil Guard', there is no question of its being set, literally, in the Sacromonte, although Lorca, aware that for centuries this hillside was 'the city of the Gypsies' by definition, surely must have had it in mind; the more so since there was often nasty trouble between the Sacromonte Gypsies and the Civil Guard, considered by the former to be their natural enemies.

The adolescent Lorca often made his way up here to listen to the Gypsies play and dance, and had many friends among them. He came to sense that they represented the deepest elements in the Andalusian psyche, and was fascinated by the mystery of their origins and the way they had maintained their identity over the centuries, despite constant persecution by the authorities (well chronicled by George Borrow in *The Gypsies of Spain*, 1841).

The *Gypsy Ballads* have been much misunderstood, many people failing to grasp that they are not so much about Gypsies as about Andalusia. The book, which became immediately famous, caused Lorca many problems, not least the generalized assumption that he himself was part Gypsy. Again and again the poet was forced to explain that his Gypsies were symbols. On one occasion he was quite explicit. 'They are ballads that seem to have different protagonists,' he said, 'but in fact have only one: Granada.'

If you have the time and energy, it's worth making the effort to visit the abbey of the Sacromonte, which stands on the slopes high above us. The road up to it begins a few hundred yards ahead on the left, through an archway. The half-kilometre ascent affords wonderful views of the valley of the Darro (Valparaíso), the Silla del Moro, the Alhambra and Generalife, and of Granada itself, and even more splendid ones are obtained from the esplanades in front, and to the side, of the main building.

The Sacromonte (Holy Mountain) is so termed because here, in some caves under the present church, a series of seemingly ancient lead tablets, mainly in Arabic, were 'discovered' in 1595; they purported to demonstrate that the Monte de Valparaíso, as it was then known, was the site of the first-century martyrdom of St Cecil, reputedly the first Bishop of Granada, and other Christians. One of the 'books' was designed to prove that Cecil was a (pre-Islamic) Arab converted to Christianity. The whole thing was later shown to have been an astonishingly elaborate hoax invented to rehabilitate the converted *moriscos* who, after the rebellion of 1568, were in very real danger of being annihilated. The issue caused a tremendous stir both in Spain and the Vatican, and for years scholarly controversy raged about whether the tablets were authentic or not. Finally they were discredited by Pope Innocent XI in 1682, seventy years after the expulsion of the *moriscos*.

You will observe that the Star of David proliferates on these buildings. In the sixteenth century the hexagonal symbol was not the sole preserve of the Jews but was also common among Christians and Muslims, with various significances. The fake lead tablets were so profusely adorned with the star that it became the emblem of the abbey that was built over the 'Holy Caves'.

The abbey, much of it now crumbling, has to my knowledge no direct Lorca associations. It does possess a fine library, however, with some Arabic manuscripts, and in its museum hangs an excellent painting by Gérard David, *The Virgin of the Rose*.

Returning now to the Cuesta del Chapiz, we turn right and continue up the steep street. In a few minutes we come to the Church of El Salvador, on our left. Twenty yards further and we arrive at the Plaza de Aliatar, on the right. From here there's a good view of San Miguel el Alto, our goal, standing on the top of its 'mount', as befits a church of St Michael.

Five streets ahead we find ourselves in front of a house with a horseshoe arch. A plaque on the wall informs us that here, in 1695, José de Mora sculpted his famous *Cristo de la Misericordia (Christ of Mercy)*. At the end of the tiny nameless alley on our right is the Casa de los Mascarones (House of Masks), home of the seventeenth-century Granadine poet Pedro Soto de Rojas, so much admired by Lorca and his friends. The stone masks that gave the building its name adorn the façade, along with the plaque in honour of the poet placed here by the Rinconcillo in 1926, the work of Hermenegildo Lanz. The house was built by Soto de Rojas on land that used to belong to Muslims. Here he created the beautiful garden that inspired his long and complicated poem *Paraíso cerrado para muchos, jardines abiertos para pocos* ('A Paradise Closed to Many, Gardens Open to Few'). In the title of the poem Lorca found the most perfect description of the authentic Granada, the Granada of the *carmen*, the inner paradise of small proportions, fountains and flowers.

We now turn into the next street on the right, San Gregorio Alto. Follow it and keep to the right. It leads us into the Placeta de Cruz de Piedra. Out of this, on the right, runs Calle San Luis, whose church of this name, a few yards down on the left, was burnt during the disturbances following the right-wing victory in the general elections of 1933 (Lorca's friend Emilia Llanos recalled that the poet was outraged by the action). The tower and shell of the building are still standing.

The first words spoken by Doña Rosita in *Doña Rosita the Spinster* are: 'And my hat? Where's my hat? The San Luis bell has already rung thirty times!' It suggests, perhaps, that in Lorca's mind Doña Rosita's *carmen* was in this parish.

The Carril de San Miguel, which leads out of the Placeta de Cruz de Piedra, to the left of the stone cross that gives its name to the square, is the starting point for our ascent to the church that inspired Lorca's famous ballad. As I warned at the beginning, keep your eyes open along here, just in case.

At the end of the street we come out on to open ground above the town. On the left are the remains of the old Arab wall, which reaches up almost to St Michael. Below us are the remains of the Church of San Luis. Beyond, the Vega and the Sierra Nevada, the Generalife, the Alhambra. This is one of the great views in Spain, and it gets even better as we climb the hill.

St Michael, Captain of the Heavenly Host, confounder of Satan, the archangel who weighs in his scales the souls of the dead, is not, as has so often been claimed, the patron saint of Granada. That honour goes to San Cecilio, who was, so far as I am aware, never mentioned by Lorca in his work. For the poet there could be no doubt: the true patron of Granada is St Michael, who presides over the city from his chapel on this hill.

Lorca's ballad to the saint is one of the panels in a poetic triptych expressing Lorca's view of the three great cities of Andalusia, each being represented by its patron saint or custodian (St Gabriel in the case of Seville, St Raphael in that of

Córdoba). Commenting on the *Gypsy Ballads*, Lorca said that his St Michael, 'king of the air, hovers over Granada, a city of torrents and mountains'.

The ballad evokes the pilgrimage that begins at dawn every Michaelmas, that is, every 29 September, and which used to be one of the most popular holidays in the Granada calendar.

Today the pilgrimage is a much watered-down affair, despite recent efforts to revive it. José Surroca y Grau, one of Lorca's teachers at Granada University, described it in a book on local customs published in 1912. On the great day stalls were erected all along the path up to the church (the path we are now following), and on the esplanade outside the chapel a wide variety of traditional cakes, buns, nuts, liqueurs, fruits and other refreshments were sold. The speciality was prickly pears (*higos chumbos*), culled from the many clumps of cacti growing on the stark hillside. From Surroca we learn that in Granada Michaelmas used to have strong amorous connotations, and that it was customary for lovers to exchange sunflowers on this occasion. Huge quantities of these were carried up to the stalls on the backs of donkeys the night before the pilgrimage. Lorca alludes to this practice in the first lines of his ballad:

Se ven desde las barandas
por el monte, monte, monte,
mulos y sombras de mulos
cargados de girasoles.

From the balustrades are seen
Going up the hill, hill, hill,
Mules and shadows of mules
Loaded with sunflowers.

The Church of St Michael, originally a hermitage, was erected on the site of an Arab tower, built to protect the wall. According to a legend, there had previously been on this site, before the Muslim invasion of AD 711, a Christian church with a miraculous olive tree that flowered and produced mature fruit all in the same day. This explains why the hill is known as the Cerro del Aceituno, the Hill of the Olive Tree. The hermitage, erected in 1673, was destroyed by the French in 1812. The present church was built soon afterwards. Today there is a reformatory attached to the church. To gain access to the latter, knock at the reformatory entrance. In my experience there has never been any problem about being allowed in.

The church is not beautiful, but the image of the saint will fascinate admirers of Lorca.

I suggest that, before entering the saint's *camarín* (recess), you view this from the aisle. It may be that Lorca's idea of composing the triptych of ballads to which I referred earlier came to him here, for you will observe that, to the right of St Michael, as seen from the aisle, there is an image of St Raphael, holding his symbol, the fish, and, to the left, one of St Gabriel, whom we recognize from his bunch of lilies, emblem of the Annunciation.

The statue of St Michael, which inspired Lorca's ballad, is the work of the sculptor Bernando Francisco de Mora, and was apparently done in 1675. We can surmise that, if it had not been so obviously androgynous, the image would not have struck Lorca so forcibly. That it did so is clear from the poem. The whole attitude of this St Michael is sexually ambiguous. He is an unconvincing Captain of the Heavenly Host, and rather than crushing Satan, represented in the guise of a grotesque cicada, seems to be caressing him with his toes. The lace bootees and spangles in which the saint is decked out add to the impression of effeminacy. Lorca captures the saint and the hot-house artificiality of his *camarín* wonderfully:

> San Miguel lleno de encajes
> en la alcoba de su torre,
> enseña sus bellos muslos
> ceñidos por los faroles.
>
> Arcángel domesticado
> en el gesto de las doce,
> finge una cólera dulce
> de plumas y ruiseñores.
> San Miguel canta en los vidrios,
> efebo de tres mil noches,
> fragante de agua colonia
> y lejano de las flores.

I translate literally:

> Saint Michael full of lace
> In the boudoir of his tower,
> shows his pretty thighs
> surrounded by the lamps.
>
> Domesticated archangel,
> In the twelve o'clock position,
> He simulates a gentle irritation
> Made of feathers and nightingales.
> Saint Michael sings behind his glass,
> Ephebe of three thousand nights,
> Fragrant with eau de cologne
> And far removed from flowers.

In seeing St Michael's church as a 'tower', Lorca may perhaps have been remembering the Arab tower that once occupied the site of the present building.

Lorca's delineation of the people who take part in his particular version of Granada's Michaelmas procession takes us close to the world of amorous repression and sadness we find in *Doña Rosita the Spinster*. The ebullient *manolas*, chewing symbolic sunflower seeds, reappear in the play. The '*damas de triste porte*' ('ladies of sad bearing') have seen better days, and their nostalgia for lost love is turning their flesh dark, a transformation also worked on that of Soledad Montoya in the 'Ballad of Black Anguish'. As for the Bishop of Manila, who officiates at a suitably ambiguous 'two-edged mass for men and women', what is he doing here? I have never been able to work it out. Nor, to my knowledge, has anyone else. Sometimes one comes across the most apparently recondite allusions in Lorca, only to discover later that there is a simple explanation. I suspect that the Bishop of Manila is a case in point, but for the moment I remain baffled.

The all but untranslatable last four lines of the poem are also difficult to interpret, although this time some light can be brought to bear:

> San Miguel, rey de los globos
> y de los números nones,

en el primor berberisco
de gritos y miradores.

Saint Michael, king of the balloons
And of uneven numbers,
Amidst the Berberesque exquisiteness
Of cries and vantage-spots.

The '*globos*' are the gas-filled balloons which used to be
released on the hillside during the Michaelmas celebrations, a
custom long since lost. And the 'uneven numbers'? This is almost
certainly an allusion to the saint's sexual ambiguity. As well as
king of the balloons that float around his sanctuary on 29
September, Lorca's St Michael presides over those people who
do not or cannot form heterosexual relationships. In defence of
this interpretation one might adduce the homosexual emperor's
search for 'The One' in *The Public*, or the composition entitled
'Little Infinite Poem', from the New York cycle, in which the
poet expresses his passionate rejection of the number two, equa-
ted with women.

Lorca himself commented on the ending of the poem. In his
lecture on Granada, with musical illustrations, 'How a City
Sings from November to November', he evokes the esplanade
in front of the church and the marvellous views obtained from
it of the Sierra Nevada. 'Granada, seen from the Hill of the
Olive, is a Berberesque delight of cries and vantage-points [*miradores*]. An indistinct music is what you hear. It's the whole
music of Granada at the same time: rivers, voices, guitar strings,
fronds, processions, a sea of fruit and the whirl of swings.'

Following the 'pilgrim route' back down the hill to the Placeta
de Cruz de Piedra, we bear right and enter the street of the same
name. It leads us some yards further on to a small Moorish
archway, the Arco de Fajalauza, which means in Arabic, according to one authority, The Gateway to the Almond Fields. From
Richard Ford's *Handbook* we know that in the nineteenth century it was from here that travellers left Granada for Murcia.

Fajalauza, the district of the Albaicín clustering around the
gate, is famous for its traditional glazed pottery, which Lorca
mentions in *Impressions and Landscapes*. You'll see it every-

where in Granada. If you want a souvenir, two nearby factories are on hand. At the end of the street in which we are now standing we enter Calle Fajalauza. Turn left and continue down to the junction with the main Murcia road 100 yards away. You will see the factories on opposite sides of the road.

Note

If you want to reach San Miguel el Alto by car you can approach it either from the centre of Granada, taking the road to Guadix and Murcia (the N-342), or else, if you have been to see the Sacromonte first, from the Albaicín. If from the latter, you leave the quarter where the Calle de Pagés – the continuation of the Cuesta del Chapiz – joins the main road to Guadix and Murcia and turn right. About 200 yards further up the road from this clearly signposted junction with the Albaicín are the ceramics factories just mentioned. Turn right here, at the traffic lights, into Calle Fajalauza and then drive up the hill to your left. After clearing the houses you'll see the church away on your right and come to the road that leads to it. By the time this book reaches your hands, the developers will have destroyed the slopes behind St Michael where, as I write, several hundred chalets are about to be built. 'Urbanización Nuevo Albaicín' the place is called. A battle was fought over the issue, as it was over the bypass, but once again the ecologists lost. St Michael's Hill has been desecrated in true Granadine fashion. The miracle, really, is that the Alhambra is still there.

The Death of a Poet

*Length: about two hours by car.*

*Distance: some 25 kilometres.*

We do not know exactly what route the car that drove Lorca to his death took out of the city, but we can make a good guess. Almost certainly they drove to the end of Calle Duquesa and, turning right into Calle del Gran Capitán, opposite the Monastery of San Jerónimo (at the back of which the Falange HQ had been installed), continued along Calle San Juan de Dios. At the end of this I imagine they crossed the continuation of the Gran Vía (today the Avenida de la Constitutión), where we ourselves did in Tour Two, and, with the Hospital Real on the left, proceeded up the Avenida del Hospicio.

If this was indeed their itinerary, they would have veered left at the end of Avenida del Hospicio into the cobbled, acacia-lined Calle Real de la Cartuja. At the end of the street several roads meet. We keep straight on (there is a signpost to Alfacar) and in a few moments come to the Carthusian Monastery (Cartuja), on our right. The church has a fine baroque interior, which was admired by Lorca. If you have time, you should certainly visit it.

Continuing on the road to Alfacar we reach a development of high-rise blocks, which are marked Osuna-1, Osuna-2, etc. After four sets of traffic lights comes the turning to the village of Víznar on the right. At the time of writing it is not very clearly signposted. (See if you can avoid driving into the block of flats that immediately precedes it.)

Whatever route the car carrying Lorca took out of Granada, it seems certain that it joined the road to Víznar here. The only other possibility is that the assassination squad drove to Víznar via the nearby village of Alfacar, but there is no evidence that they went this considerably longer way round.

In 1936 this road was little more than a cart track, and as late as the 1970s its surface was appalling. It must have been a rough ride for Lorca and Dióscoro Galindo González that night.

As the car climbs up towards Víznar the valley of the phantom River Beiro is on our right. As I said earlier, it is almost always without water. On the other side of the 'river', a few kilometres further on, rise the chimneys of the gunpowder factory of El Fargue, which played such a vital part in the Civil War.

It takes about fifteen minutes, driving carefully, to reach Víznar. The last stretch of the road is steep.

When you enter the village, bear immediately right and stop in the little fountain-embellished square. Here, in the palace of the eighteenth-century prelate Archbishop Moscoso y Peralta, the Falange established a stronghold on the outbreak of the war. It was evident to the rebels that the village was to become a position of considerable importance in the struggle to resist Republican incursions from the hilly country to the north-east of the capital, and they decided to make Víznar as impregnable as possible.

The Falangist contingent was commanded by a young army officer, Captain José María Nestares, who had been seconded to the police security department in Granada before the rising. Nestares loathed the Republic and had been one of the most active conspirators in the town. In Víznar he had powers of life and death.

Just inside the entrance to the palace there is a plaque recording its role during the war. It reads:

The barracks of the First Granada Spanish Falange was established in this palace on 29 July 1936. Inside these walls it grew to become the First Bandera, then the First Tercio of the Traditionalist Spanish Falange of Granada, which in fierce combats maintained the security of our capital against the Marxist onslaught.

Víznar was not only a military position. It was also one of the principal places where the Granada rebels dispatched their prisoners. 'Execution' is too good a word for what happened here. 'Assassination', often preceded by torture, comes closer to the mark. Nestares was in constant touch with Valdés, and every night cars would arrive from the Civil Government building and the villages of the surrounding countryside with batches of 'undesirables'. The vehicles from Granada had first to pass in front of Moscoso's palace, where they would usually exchange papers with Falange HQ before setting off up the hill in the direction of Alfacar.

The car that brought Lorca and Galindo González probably stopped here for a moment, although no witness has ever come forward with evidence on this point.

From the square there is only one road they could then have taken, the one that hugs the palace wall and climbs out of the village. Above Víznar the ground levels out. A plaque on our right informed us until recently that we were entering the Avenida de los Mártires, or Avenue of the Martyrs. It was of bronze. The original, more fragile, plaque was smashed by unidentified vandals, presumably right-wing extremists outraged that the Socialist Town Council of Víznar should have dared to honour in this way the hundreds of 'enemies of Spain' killed just down the road. What has happened to the bronze plaque I do not know. Perhaps the extremists also removed it. Maybe it will have been replaced by the time this book is published.

Away below us spreads the broad expanse of the Vega, with, at its edge, the stark Sierra Elvira, whose treeless slopes form a brusque contrast with the lushness of the fertile plain; directly ahead rises the Sierra de Alfacar, with a cross on its highest point.

A hundred yards on, just before a sharp corner, there is space enough on the left to park the car (be as careful as you can that nothing is coming, and pull over quickly). Immediately below the road, beside a delightful *acequia*, or watercourse, are the scant remains of the building where Lorca spent his last hours (it was demolished in the 1970s, see Plate 7B). You will certainly want to clamber down to them.

In the days of the Republic there was a spacious house here, Villa Concha, built over and around an old mill (some of the old mill-stones were still lying beside the *acequia* on my last visit). During the summer months Villa Concha served as a hostel for schoolchildren from Granada and was known to the locals, accordingly, as 'La Colonia'. When the Falangists converted Víznar into a military position at the end of July 1936 the children were sent home and La Colonia was turned into a makeshift prison. Here the cars came each day and night with new loads of victims. A building associated with happiness and holidays had suddenly become a mansion of death.

A party of freemasons and other 'undesirables' was brought here from Granada to dig the unmarked graves. Some of these men were later shot themselves. As for the killers, most were 'Black Squad' volunteers, but there were also some Republican policemen – Assault Guards – forced to participate in the shootings as a punishment for their initial lack of support for the Nationalist cause. From time to time new volunteers for the job appeared.

The victims were locked in downstairs until the early morning, and the parish priest of Víznar was usually at hand to take their last confessions, if they so desired. Upstairs were quarters at the disposal of the men who took part in the shootings.

At least two women were in La Colonia during the early months of the repression: María Luisa Alcalde González, an attractive and prominent left-winger from Granada whom Nestares was protecting and who cooked for the men, and an English girl, Frances Turner, said by some to have served as a nurse in Víznar and by others sometimes to have taken part in the killings. The English Consul, William Davenhill, did not like to talk about the young woman, who lived near him with her family and was celebrated in Granada for her equestrian skills, but Gerald Brenan prised some information out of him and mentions her obliquely in his chapter on Granada in *The Face of Spain* (1950):

How catching the hysteria was may be seen from the fact that an ordinary English girl, whose parents were living in Granada, donned the uniform of the Falange, stuck a revolver in her belt and boasted that, like other Spanish *señoritas*, she had taken part in executions and shot men with her own hand. Later, when the European war broke out, she returned to England and joined an ambulance squad.

The killings normally took place just before dawn, but sometimes during the day as well. The gravediggers would bury the dead where they lay, all around this wide valley. Not infrequently they found themselves staring at the corpse of a friend or relative.

We know from several witnesses that Lorca spent his last hours at La Colonia. Especially important is the testimony of José Jover Tripaldi. This young man from a petty aristocratic background was twenty-two when the war began, and holidaying in Víznar. In order to avoid being called up he asked Captain Nestares, a friend of the family, to let him work with him in some capacity. Nestares agreed, and arranged for the lad to be given guard duty at the Colonia. He was there the night that Lorca arrived. A fervent Catholic, it was Jover Tripaldi's custom to inform the victims that they would be taken the following morning to work on fortifications, or to repair roads. Then, as the moment for the shootings drew near, he used to tell them the terrible truth. This he saw as charity. If the prisoners wanted, they could then ask the parish priest to confess them and give the guards a last message for their families (not, one imagines, always delivered).

According to Jover Tripaldi, when Lorca was told that he was going to be shot, he refused confession at first but then, as the moment came nearer, decided that he wanted to take it after all. But the priest had already left. The younger man, seeing the poet's deep distress, assured him that, if he asked God sincerely to forgive his sins, he would receive absolution. He helped Federico with the prayer beginning 'I, sinner . . .', which the poet only half remembered from his childhood. 'My mother taught it to me,' the poet murmured, 'but I've almost completely forgotten it.' Jover Tripaldi told me that Lorca seemed more tranquil once he had prayed.

With Lorca and Galindo González were two small-time bull-fighters from Granada, Joaquín Arcollas Cabezas and Francisco Galadí Melgar. Both were militant anarchists and had been among those who most vociferously demanded arms for the people when the rising was imminent. Their capture (in the Albaicín) meant certain death.

From the site of La Colonia the road winds on around the

valley in the direction of Alfacar, accompanied by the water-course which, half a mile or so ahead, passes over a narrow aqueduct, now further below us, where the road loops sharply to the left.

Immediately in front of us a wedge-shaped wood of tall pines stretches back up the hillside towards the first rocky outcrops of the Sierra de Alfacar. This is the ill-famed *barranco*, or gully, of Víznar where lie the bodies of most of the victims of the system operating at La Colonia. Shallow graves were dug all over the slope (there were no trees here then), the bodies were tossed in and a thin covering of stones and soil was thrown over them. When Gerald Brenan visited the spot in 1949 he found that 'the entire area was pitted with low hollows and mounds, at the head of each of which had been placed a small stone.' By the early 1950s the evidence afforded by these head-stones had been removed, however, and pines had been planted, presumably to mask the outlines of the graves which, none the less, were in many cases still clearly visible fifteen years later.

I suggest you scramble up the pebbly slope and view the place. The largest pit in the *barranco*, which must hold at least a hundred bodies, was dug in what in summer is a dry, rush-edged dip and in winter becomes a pool. You will have no difficulty in finding it. It is in the middle of the pines and has been marked with an improvised cross of stones. Every 19 August a pilgrimage of Lorca-lovers makes its way here on the anniversary of his death. Poems are recited and pinned to the trees; there are tears.

In the first days of the repression, the killings were not carried out in the *barranco* but in the olive groves that used to clothe the valley more thickly than they do now. Lorca was one of those early victims, and contrary to what has often been said is not buried here. So let us continue on our way.

The road now curves on around the valley, with the *acequia* still running beside it. Soon we come, on our right, to the Parque Federico García Lorca, created to preserve the spot where Lorca and his fellow-victims were shot and, at the same time, in a generous gesture, to honour the memory of all those who died in the Civil War.

On the other side of the road, just before the park, is an ugly block of holiday flats, El Caracolar.

In 1936 and right up to the 1950s there were hardly any buildings in these parts. Then the developers began to move in. Granada County Council acquired the land for the memorial park in the nick of time. Had they failed, there would probably now be villas on top of Lorca's remains.

There are things about the park that you almost certainly won't like, such as the monumental entrance and the awful fountain just inside it, on the right. But at least the olive tree beside which the poet was shot has been carefully preserved, and the ground around it left almost exactly in its original state. It is at the end of the park, to the left of the entrance, beside the other gate.

The four prisoners were driven here before sunrise on either 18 or 19 August 1936 – it has not been possible to establish the date with certainty, although the earlier one now looks more likely. There was no moon; Lorca, lunar poet that he was, did not have even that consolation. No trustworthy account of the poet's last moments has come down to us. There is no record of his words, if he spoke any; none of any request. Did he perceive the almost uncanny parallel between his fate and that of his heroine Mariana Pineda? Did he think about his mother, about his last lover Rafael Rodríguez Rapún, remember the many lines (there were so many) in which he had expressed his horror of death and perhaps even his premonitions about his own assassination? It is terrible for those of us who love the man and his work not to know the answers to such questions.

According to two independent sources, the poet was not killed outright by the first shots, and had to be finished off by a *coup de grâce*. Other oral accounts, not verifiable but convincing enough, suggest that he was beaten and reviled before being shot. Among the assassins, almost certainly, was one of Ramón Ruiz Alonso's accomplices, Juan Luis Trescastro, who boasted later that morning in Granada that he had just helped to kill Lorca, firing, for good measure, 'two bullets into his arse for being a queer'. Such was the mentality of the local bourgeoisie criticized by the poet in the Madrid daily *El Sol*, Spain's leading liberal newspaper, two months earlier.

A few minutes after the killings the gravedigger arrived, a young communist called Manuel Castilla Blanco whom Captain Nestares was protecting at La Colonia. The lad immediately recognized the bullfighters, noticed not without surprise that another of the victims had a wooden leg, and observed that the last one had on a loose tie, 'you know, the sort artists wear'. He buried them in a narrow trench, one on top of the other, beside the same olive tree that today guards the simple granite stone recording what happened here. When Castilla returned to La Colonia they told him that the man with the wooden leg was a schoolteacher from a nearby village, and the one with the loose tie the poet Federico García Lorca.

Before Lorca was shot that morning at least 280 people had already been killed in Granada cemetery, and the real total for the city and the surrounding villages was much higher. The Fascists were determined to liquidate all their left-wing opponents, and so far as they were concerned Lorca was just one more 'Red intellectual', albeit a particularly obnoxious one.

The guitarist Angel Barrios, Lorca's friend from the days of the Rinconcillo, was spending the summer in Víznar when the war broke out. Hearing the terrible news of the poet's assassination, he made inquiries and discovered where the killing had taken place. A few days later he visited the spot, and found that lime had been thrown over the grave. The whole area stank of rotting corpses.

Did Lorca know that he was about to be shot in a place with rich poetic associations? I believe he may have done. Two hundred yards further down the road on the left, in the direction of Alfacar, is the spring known as the Fuente Grande, or Big Fountain, which I am certain will fascinate you. Lorca must have known it, since it has long been famous in Granada.

In Lorca's day this whole area was almost completely barren and there were practically no buildings around the pool. Since the 1950s the spot has become increasingly popular, however, and it has now lost most of its former charm. Note the appalling little church above the pool, with three crosses that look more

like missiles waiting to be fired by remote control than symbols
of Christian love.

The Muslims, intrigued by the bubbles that rise continually
to the surface of the pool, called it Ainadamar, 'The Fountain
of Tears', and in the eleventh century began the construction of
a canal to carry the water to Granada. Almost a thousand years
later the watercourse still flows to the city, looping around the
valley to Víznar, where it used to move the wheel of La Colonia
(Lorca must have listened to its rush that last night), dropping
down to El Fargue, where it feeds the gunpowder factory, and
skirting the hills to the Albaicín, which it supplied until quite
recently.

Ainadamar was more vigorous in the past than it is now,
however, for Richard Ford (who may not have come here himself) described it as 'a vast spring of water which bubbles up in
a column several feet high'.

The Muslims admired the loveliness of the pool's surroundings, and a sizeable colony of summer residences soon arose in
the vicinity. No vestiges of them remain, perhaps as a result
of an earthquake, but several compositions in Arabic praising
Ainadamar's beauty survive, among them one by the judge, poet
and historian Abū'l-Barakāt al-Bakafīqī, who died in AD 1372
(the translation is by my friend, the Arabist James Dickie):

Is it my separation from Ainadamar, stopping the pulsation of my
blood, which has dried up the flow of tears from the well of my eyes?

Its waters moan in sadness like the moaning of one who, enslaved
by love, has lost his heart.

Beside it the birds sing melodies comparable to those of the Mausilī,*
reminding me of the now distant past into which I entered in my youth;
and the moons of that place,† beautiful as Joseph, would make every
Muslim abandon his faith for that of love.

It seems appropriate that Ainadamar, the Fountain of Tears
sung about by the Islamic poets of Granada, should continue
to bubble up its clear waters close to the last resting place of

---

* A reference to Isḥāq al-Mausilī (that is, from Mosul), the most famous of
all Arab musicians.
† In plain words, the local women.

the greatest poet ever born in this part of Spain. Had the killers known of the spring's literary associations, perhaps, as a last quirk of sadism, they might have chosen some more banal spot in which to carry out their foul task. Luckily they did not.

To return to Granada from here the best route is to drop down into Alfacar, which has grown hugely, and unbeautifully, over the last few years. The only remarkable thing about the place is its bread, long celebrated in Granada. Follow the signposting to Granada. Once we have traversed the straggling town the road soon leads us back to the point where we branched off to Víznar.

## TOUR NINE Fuente Vaqueros (The Poet's Birthplace in the Vega), Valderrubio and Moclín

*Distance: about 100 kilometres including Moclín, 70 without.*

*Length: some five hours by car, one less if you don't visit Moclín.*

*To avoid disappointment it's advisable to telephone the Casa-Museo Federico García Lorca in Fuente Vaqueros before setting off for the village and to check on visiting hours. The number is: (958) 44.64.53.*

*For the full tour a car is essential. If you only want to visit Fuente Vaqueros, see the note at the end of the tour. There are direct buses every hour from the Avenida de los Andaluces, next to the railway station (the trip takes about twenty minutes and precise timetable details can be supplied by the Casa-Museo when you ring about visiting hours).*

When I went to Fuente Vaqueros for the first time, in the spring of 1965, I travelled on the little tram that in those days still plied the 18 kilometres that separate the village from Granada. It was a delightful, snail-pace trip through the fields, with stops at all the villages en route. Alas, the tram is no more.

I recommend that you make your way first to Sante Fe, 10 kilometres from Granada on the N-342 to Loja, Málaga and Seville. Sante Fe (Holy Faith) was built by Ferdinand and Isabella during the siege of Granada in 1491 – in eighty days it is said – and preserves its original square shape, based on the plan of a Roman encampment. If you stand in the middle of the street beside the main square you find yourself at the centre of a cross from which you can see each of the four gateways, three of which still have their original chapels over them. In Santa Fe, at the end of 1491, the Catholic monarchs and the emissary of the last Moorish king of Granada, Boabdil, signed the terms

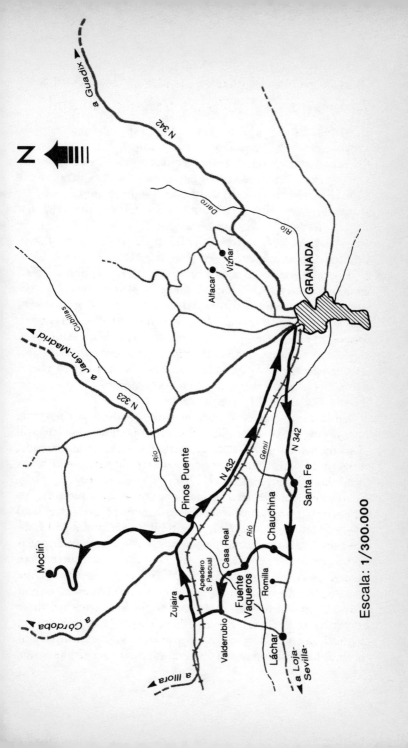

Escala: 1/300.000

whereby the city was to be surrendered. These terms were favourable to the Muslims – and soon broken. The original document is preserved in the Granada City Archive, housed, as I pointed out in Tour Seven, in the Casa de los Córdova at the foot of the Cuesta del Chapiz. It has been splendidly reproduced in facsimile by Granada Town Council.

Sante Fe is famous for another reason. It was here, on 17 April 1492, shortly after Granada was handed over to the Christians, that Ferdinand and Isabella signed with Christopher Columbus the contract (which they also failed to honour) that led to the discovery of America. The following 3 August the *Santa María*, the *Pinta* and the *Niña* sailed from Palos de la Frontera, reaching the New World on 12 October.

No doubt the young Lorca was well informed from an early age about the historic role of Santa Fe. His maternal grand-parents were from the town, and as a child he passed through here on his way to Granada in the 'old carriage' mentioned in a letter to his friend Melchor Fernández Almagro.

We now continue on the N-342. In the distance, on our right, rises the Sierra de Parapanda, which, as Richard Ford points out in his *Handbook*, is 'the barometer of the Vega' (I quoted this passage in Tour Three). When a cloud settles on Parapanda, it rains even though God doesn't want it to, says the proverb. Lorca knew the saying well, and makes one of his characters in *Mariana Pineda* quote it. Today Parapanda, from whose bare, rocky top there is a fabulous view of the fertile plain, is crowned by a tall television mast.

Some 5 kilometres from Santa Fe we turn right at the sign to the village of Chauchina, a kilometre down the road.

In Chauchina lived the Gypsy prototype of Lorca's Antonio Torres Heredia, 'son and grandson of the Camborios', one of the most colourful characters in the *Gypsy Ballads*. Luis Cortés Heredia by name, his father ran a butcher's shop in the village. Luis was famous in the Vega for his good looks, style and success with women. He played the guitar brilliantly, and according to Aurelia González García, one of Lorca's favourite cousins in Fuente Vaqueros, no party was complete without him. Then, one June night in 1904, as he was returning home, perhaps after a binge, he fell off his horse and was killed. Federico was six then and must have heard about the tragedy. In his mind Luis became a mythical figure and, one day, was reborn as the Gypsy hero Antonio Torres Heredia, that 'living coin that can never be struck again' murdered by his jealous cousins.

During Lorca's childhood Chauchina had another picturesque character in the person of its mayor, a man celebrated for his eccentricities. According to one of the García Lorcas' neighbours in Fuente Vaqueros, the mayor in *The Shoemaker's Prodigious Wife* owes much to him.

Chauchina, then, has its importance in Lorca's world.

Following the signs to Fuente Vaqueros we soon find ourselves deep in the Vega among maize and tobacco fields and dense poplar groves (the latter, so typical of this region, are mainly used for making boxes). In a few minutes we arrive at an inconspicuous bridge over the Genil. The river has very little water in summer and its dry bed always reminds me of Lorca's ballad 'La Casada infidel' ('The Faithless Wife'), the action of which, as the poet once explained, takes place during a '*noche de vega alta y junco en penumbra*' ('a night of deep *vega* and reed in shadow').

Before we enter Fuente Vaqueros, which is just across the river, I want to show you something special: an old Moorish watchtower where Lorca played as a child. Not many people know about this, and really I shouldn't divulge the secret, but still . . . So let's take the little unsurfaced road that leads away on our left, immediately before the bridge. Try, I beg you, not to raise too much dust as you drive along this. Ideally one would never come here in a car.

In the distance, once again, rises Parapanda, and on the other side of the river we see the first houses of Fuente Vaqueros. After a kilometre and a half the poplar groves come to an end and across the fields, to our left, is the tower, reached along a lane that leads to the village of Romilla, which we can see in the background (there are one or two little paths off to the left before this one, so use your instinct).

Lorca explains in his early autobiographical text, 'My Village', about his childhood in Fuente Vaqueros, that according to the locals the tower was inhabited by a giant lizard that violated the tombs in the little cemetery of Romilla and ate the female corpses but 'respected' the male. When his companions took him there, he says, he was terrified.

The tower is known as the Torre de Roma, a name that requires some explanation.

The Muslims of Granada were expert horticulturists and hydraulic engineers, and in the Vega they created an intricate irrigation system, still largely in use, which improved notably on that left by the Romans. For 700 years the Vega was a paradise, one Arab author reckoning it 'superior in extent and fertility to the Ghauttah, or the valley of Damascus' (I take the quotation from Richard Ford). But with the fall of Granada to the Christians, the plain entered on a period of prolonged decline. Little by little the agricultural prosperity of the region dwindled, and the reversal culminated with the expulsion of the *moriscos*, or converted Moors, in 1609.

The Torre de Roma marks the edge, approximately, of a large estate in the centre of the Vega, the Soto de Roma, that belonged to the Muslim kings of Granada. Why 'Roma'? The experts disagree about the origins of the word (there appears to be no connection with the Italian homonym), although it seems most likely that it derives from an Arabic root for 'Christian'. This etymology is supported by the tradition according to which Florinda, the alluring daughter of Count Julián, the traitor blamed for opening the gates of Spain to the Muslims, is said to have lived in the nearby village of Romilla. As for 'Soto', it is from the Latin *saltus* and means 'meadow', 'estate' or 'wood'. It appears, then, that Soto de Roma may have the sense of 'The Estate (Meadow, Wood) of the Christian Girl'.

Richard Ford opted for another, I think less convincing, etymology, stating that 'Roma' derives from the Arabic for 'pomegranate'. For him, Soto de Roma meant 'The Wood of the Pomegranates'. He supported this derivation by pointing out that in Granada you could still eat a delicious pomegranate salad called '*ensalada romana*'. (I have searched for it in vain.)

Ferdinand and Isabella distributed the fertile land of the Vega – all 2000 square kilometres of it – among their nobles. But they took good care to reserve the Soto de Roma for the sole use of themselves and their descendants. To the estate's name was added from this time the title of *Real Sitio*, or Royal Demesne.

In the sixteenth century the Soto was very thickly wooded, and teemed with game. Ginés Pérez de Hita, author of *The Civil Wars of Granada*, published in 1595, refers to the density of the place's vegetation. 'Unless you know the paths well you can easily get lost,' he wrote. Five hundred years later it is still possible to go astray in the woods of the Soto, now mostly poplar groves (the other species have long since been ousted).

For three centuries the Soto de Roma remained in the hands of the Crown, undergoing only minimal agricultural exploitation and serving almost exclusively to satisfy the passion for hunting of the royal family who, during their infrequent visits, lodged at the Casa Real, or Royal House, erected where the Rivers Cubillas and Genil used to meet, about half a mile from Fuente Vaqueros. (The Genil formerly ran to the north of Fuente Vaqueros. But in 1827, after particularly torrential rains, the river burst its banks near Santa Fe and changed course, moving to the south of the village, where we find it today.)

Perhaps just a little more history. In 1765 Charles III gave the estate to Richard Wall, the son of Irish immigrants, who had been Spanish Ambassador to the Court of St James and Secretary of State during the years 1754–64. In the tiny village of Fuente Vaqueros (Fountain of the Cowmen), this Richard Wall (by all accounts a charming individual) began the construction of the Parish Church of Our Lady of the Annunciation, but he died, in 1777, before he could see the work completed. The estate then reverted to the Crown, being granted not long afterwards to the wretched Manuel Godoy, Charles IV's minister and lover of his plump wife, María Luisa, so wickedly portrayed by Goya. Godoy never visited the Soto de Roma, and when he fell from favour in 1805, after Nelson's victory at Trafalgar, and went into exile, it returned once again to the Crown.

Four years later the fortunes of the Soto de Roma took a strange turn indeed. In 1812 Arthur Wellesley, the first Duke of Wellington, conqueror of Napoleon at Salamanca, became the idol of Spain. As an expression of gratitude for his contribution to the defeat of the French (which the Spaniards have tended to play down), the Liberal Parliament of Cádiz conferred on Wellesley, in 1813, the title of Duke of Ciudad Rodrigo, and granted to him and his successors in perpetuity, not only the Soto de Roma but another estate, situated on the rising terrain to the north-west, called Molino de Rey (King's Mill). For more than a hundred years the Soto, once hunted over by the Muslims, was to belong, lock, stock and barrel, to the Wellesley family.

In 1813 the Soto de Roma boasted about 700 inhabitants living in several villages, the largest of which was Fuente Vaqueros. Sir Arthur never visited his estates in Granada, which were run during the nineteenth century by a series of agents, usually incompetent, normally absent and almost always corrupt. One exception was the first administrator, General O'Lawlor, who, as one would guess from his name, was of Irish descent like Wall. O'Lawlor had been Wellington's aide-de-camp during the Peninsular campaign, and had served him loyally. Now he combined his post as the duke's agent with that of Captain General of Granada. In 1831 Richard Ford spent a few days in Fuente Vaqueros with O'Lawlor. In his *Handbook* he made the point, commenting on the labours of Wall and O'Lawlor, that the Soto twice owed its restoration 'to Irish care'.

Until the end of the nineteenth century, when the Genil was contained within embankments, the Soto was subject to frequent flooding. Each autumn, when the rains began, both the river and its tributary the Cubillas overflowed, as did the irrigation channels of the estate. The fragile wooden bridges spanning the rivers used invariably to be swept away in the deluge and, the rivers themselves being unfordable, communication between the tenants and the outside world, as well as between them and the land they worked, would be severed.

As a result of the humidity of the area, 'La Fuente', as Fuente Vaqueros is universally known in the Vega, was considered an unhealthy place until the beginning of the twentieth century.

Horacio Hammick, friend and subsequently agent of the second Duke of Wellington, attempted to visit Fuente Vaqueros in the autumn of 1854. The rains prevented him from doing so. In the autumn of 1858 he had better luck, and after numerous difficulties managed to reach the village. He found it and the Soto generally in a state of the utmost dilapidation. Many of the inhabitants were undergoing desperate hardship; the place was full of half-naked beggars; work on the land had come to a standstill; there was a dire shortage of bread; many people were dying of fever. 'And they earnestly entreated us,' wrote Hammick in his book *The Duke of Wellington's Spanish Estate. A Personal Narrative* (1885), 'to acquaint their lord [ . . . ] with their miserable condition.'

But if the floods brought hunger and misery each winter to the Soto de Roma, it was also true that the soil of the estate owed its fertility to the carpets of loam spread over the area down the centuries by the Genil and the Cubillas. The earth of Fuente Vaqueros, owing to the proximity of the village to both rivers, was, and remains, particularly rich, as Lorca liked to point out whenever he was given the opportunity.

The population of the Soto increased throughout the nineteenth century. By 1868 it had grown to some 3,000 souls. Such rapid expansion was due in part to the agricultural innovations gradually introduced by the English agents. Another stimulus was a strong industrial demand at the time for hemp and flax, both of which flourished in the Vega (Richard Ford says that the hemp of the Vega 'is the finest in the world'). Hammick was of the opinion that the system whereby the duke's tenants could let and sublet their holdings almost *ad infinitum* also assisted the population explosion.

Towards 1880 another, much more decisive factor came to bear on the situation, promoting the development and enrichment not only of the Soto de Roma but of the Vega as a whole: the discovery that sugar-beet could be grown here very successfully. Soon the Vega was a hive of activity. Tall-chimneyed factories for the processing of the beet sprang up (we shall see some of them later) and many landowners made rapid fortunes, among them Federico García Rodríguez, the poet's father. The loss of Cuba to the United States in 1898 came as a further boost to this new industry, for it meant that the importation of cheap sugar from the island had come to an end. The plain was booming, and by the time Lorca was born in Fuente Vaqueros on 5 June 1898 his father had become one of the wealthiest men in the village.

That's enough background to the Soto de Roma.

The Cubillas joins the Genil not far from the Torre de Roma. If you want to see this charming spot, turn left when you regain the bank of the Genil. When I was last there the state of the road was such that it was only possible to reach the meeting of the waters on foot. You'll enjoy the brief stroll.

We now return to the bridge, turn left and proceed to Fuente Vaqueros, which we reach in a few minutes.

The village square has been much spruced up recently and has nothing in common with the meadow where Lorca played as a child and where the women would stretch out the clothes they had washed in the fountain that gives Fuente Vaqueros its name (the fountain isn't the same either).

Lorca was born in No. 4 Calle de la Trinidad, at the top left corner of the square as we look towards the monument to the poet, done by Cayetano Aníbal. The house has been bought and restored by Granada County Council. Officially termed the Casa-Museo Federico García Lorca, it was opened to the public on 29 July 1986, since when many thousands of visitors have made their way here. The entrance is at the back of the house, in Calle Manuel de Falla.

Federico García Rodríguez, the poet's father, had married his first wife, Matilde Palacios Ríos, in 1880. Like him, she was a native of Fuente Vaqueros. Her father was well-off, and owned land of his own outside the Soto de Roma (inside the boundaries of the estate all the land was rented from the duke). It was an advantageous match, then, for the twenty-year-old Federico. Matilde's father was pleased with her choice of husband, and built the couple this spacious house.

All seemed set fair for them, and the discovery that Matilde was unable to have children must have come as a terrible blow. Then, on 4 October 1894, fourteen years after her marriage, Matilde died suddenly from what her death certificate terms an 'intestinal obstruction'. The house passed for life to her widower, as well as a considerable sum of money. Years later, as he was writing *Yerma* and mulling over the terrible frustration of a village woman unable to have a baby, Lorca may well have had the unfortunate Matilde in mind. Once he said that during his childhood he had been obsessed by the photographs 'of that other woman who could have been my mother'.

The director of the Casa-Museo, since it opened in 1986, has been the Granadine poet Juan de Loxa, the perfect man for the job. I hope that he is still in charge when this book comes your way, and that you meet him. His guided tour of the Casa-Museo and its *lorquiana*, which includes the poet's cot, first editions, videos, a library and the manuscript of the Argentinian version of the *Retablillo de don Cristóbal (Don Cristóbal's Puppet Show)*, is not to be missed.

Note, on the stairs up to the loft, where exhibitions are held, the print of the *Cristo del Paño* of Moclín, which we visit later in this tour. The annual pilgrimage to this miracle-working picture is famous in Granada and partly inspired *Yerma*.

In 1902 or 1903 the García Lorca family moved to another house at No. 2 Calle de la Iglesia, the first street on the right back down the square. The house stood on the right-hand corner and was pulled down some years ago to make way for a new building. In his early prose piece 'My Village', Lorca recalls wistfully the games he used to organize in the attic. One gets the impression from his account that, by orchestrating these activities himself and giving all the orders, he was compensating for his marked lack of physical agility. Be this as it may, the poet never forgot the games and songs of his childhood in Fuente Vaqueros. They are part of the bedrock on which he built his work.

You should make a point of visiting the parish church, at the end of the street. Here, on 11 June 1898, the future poet was baptized Federico del Sagrado Corazón de Jesus, Federico of the Sacred Heart of Jesus. Vicenta Lorca, his schoolteacher mother, was a practising Catholic and Federico was often taken to the church, whose liturgy, processions and festivities impressed him deeply. In 'My Village' he remembers with affection the little tower of the building, 'so low that it hardly stands out from the rest of the houses, so that when the bells peal they seem to emanate from the bowels of the earth'. Behind the altar stood a smiling image of the Virgin of Good Love (La Virgen del Buen Amor), 'always laughing and a little silly with her tin crown, stars and spangles'. This image has since disappeared, and no one I have talked to in the village has been able to tell me why.

Fascinated by the rituals of the Church, the young Federico soon began to imitate them in his own way. One of his favourite games was 'saying Mass'. In the back yard of the house there was a low wall on which the child would place a statue of the Virgin and some roses cut from the garden. Servants, family, friends – all were roped in and made to sit down in front of the wall while Federico, wrapped in an odd assortment of discarded garments culled from the attic, would 'say Mass' with enormous conviction. Before beginning he used to impose a condition: it was the congregation's obligation to weep during the sermon.

One day a travelling puppet theatre arrived in La Fuente. Federico had never seen a puppet show, and his excitement was intense while the little theatre was being assembled in the square. According to a family friend, Carmen Ramos, who had been Federico's wetnurse, such was the impact of the show that the next day an improvised puppet theatre took the place of the 'altar' on the garden wall.

In that first contact with the tradition of Andalusian puppetry we may be permitted to see, I think, the origins not only of Lorca's love of the genre (he himself wrote several puppet plays) but of his later enthusiasm for the work of La Barraca, the itinerant university theatre which he directed from 1932.

The people of Fuente Vaqueros had a reputation in the Vega for their love of books, a love shared by almost all Federico's family. How can this phenomenon be accounted for? It is possible that it had something to do with the fact that La Fuente belonged to the Duke of Wellington, a circumstance that set the villagers apart from the rest of the inhabitants of the plain and gave them, through their contact with the Protestant English, a broader view of life and the world. On the other hand the locals resented the English considerably for, despite having to make only minimal payments (always in kind) to the landowner, it rankled to be tenants of a foreign nobleman, no matter how distinguished the contribution of his great forebear to the well-being of Spain.

As for the English, they had a pretty poor opinion of their tenants. They did not trust them. They spoke of the 'doubtful reputation' of the village; of left-wing agitators who operated there to stir up trouble. The Wellesleys believed, apparently, that in the eighteenth century Charles III had settled the area with convicts, and that this accounted for a 'mutinous streak' in the population, always liable to break out. I have found no evidence in support of the claim, however, and the alleged rebelliousness of La Fuente needs no such atavistic explanation. It was simply that the villagers felt humiliated by their thraldom to the foreigner (from which they were freed in the early 1920s).

But whatever the reasons, the fact remains that Fuente Vaqueros was different from the other villages of the Vega. Liberal, 'a bolshie lot, always against authority' (as one disgruntled English agent put it), and unconcerned about religious matters, these people were surprisingly open and progressive. The García clan was a case in point.

Lorca was about seven when the family moved to his 'second' village, Asquerosa. He himself said repeatedly that his childhood in Fuente Vaqueros made an indelible impression on him. When the Republic came in 1931, a Socialist council was elected in the village. One of the first things they did was to give the poet's name to Calle de la Iglesia, where he had lived from the age of four. (When the rebels took Fuente Vaqueros at the beginning of the Civil War the street reverted to its old name.) Lorca came for the ceremony and, in his speech of thanks, expressed his gratitude to the village for making him a poet:

You may believe me when I say that I am deeply grateful, and that, when in Madrid or any other place they ask me [ . . . ] to say where I was born, I always reply that I saw the first light of day in Fuente Vaqueros, so that the fame that may come to me may also come to this delightful, modern and liberal village of La Fuente [ . . . ] It's built on water. On all sides murmur the irrigation channels and grow the tall poplars where in summer the wind plays its soft melodies. At its very centre there's a fountain which wells up incessantly, and beyond its rooftops rise the blue mountains around the Vega – but far-off, distant, as if they preferred that their rocky slopes should not reach here, where a rich, fertile soil enables all sorts of fruits to thrive.

Lorca's father was the eldest of nine brothers and sisters, all of whom married and had children. As a result, Federico had more than forty cousins and an intense social life, growing up surrounded by affection. The Garcías, who had been living in Fuente Vaqueros for generations, were talented people, with a great flair for folk song and poetry which Federico inherited and refined. Those early childhood years in Fuente Vaqueros and the surrounding countryside were always to remain within him as a constant present, seemingly impervious to the action of time. When he was in Argentina in 1934 he told a journalist:

I love the countryside. I feel myself linked to it in all my emotions. My earliest childhood memories have the flavour of the earth. The meadows, the fields, have done wonders for me. The wild animals of the countryside, the livestock, the people living on the land, all these have a fascination that very few people grasp. Were this not so I could not have written *Blood Wedding*. My first emotional experiences are associated with the land and the work on the land. That's why there's at the heart of my life what psychoanalysts would call an 'agrarian complex'.

A year later, back in Spain, he told another journalist:

Above all, I love simplicity. I learnt the simple way of life in my childhood, in the village. Because I wasn't born in Granada, you know, but in a village called Fuente Vaqueros.

Having finished our visit to Fuente Vaqueros, we take the straight, tree-lined avenue that leads out of the square behind the monument to the poet. This is the road to Asquerosa, today Valderrubio, to which the García Lorcas moved around 1907.

About half a kilometre ahead a lane on the right turns down to the Fuente Vaqueros cemetery. If you have time you might care to pay it a brief visit, but you'll have to ask the way unless it has been signposted since my last visit. Many of Lorca's relatives are buried here.

A further half kilometre along the road to Valderrubio brings us to the Casa Real, on our left. It has recently been restored and is in private hands. When Horacio Hammick visited Fuente Vaqueros in 1858 he found the place in ruins: there were no doors or windows; the walls were cracked; and the upper floor was occupied by Gypsies. Richard Ford had spent several days here in 1831 with the Duke's agent, O'Lawlor, and did some fine drawings of the place, then in better repair.

Shortly after the Casa Real we arrive at the bridge over the Cubillas. The river marks the western boundary of the Soto de Roma and its banks are thick with poplars. This was one of the magical spots where Lorca played as a child, and I advise a stroll through the woods. The atmosphere has changed little since the days when the future poet roamed here.

We come out of the *choperas* (poplar groves) on to a broad stretch of Vega. To the right, across fields that used to belong to the poet's father, rises a tall chimney. It belonged to the San Pascual sugar-beet refinery, in which Don Federico was a leading shareholder (the factory has been shut long since and today there is pig-breeding on the premises).

Taking the rough, unsurfaced road that, 50 yards from the poplars, leads in the direction of the chimney, we pass the old factory and arrive at the bridge that crosses the railway from Granada to Loja and Málaga. On our right we see a derelict station. This is the Apeadero de San Pascual, which we can reach on foot from the road (*apeadero* means, literally, 'getting-down-spot'). In several letters to his friends Lorca gives Apeadero de San Pascual as his summer address. From here the views of the Vega and the Sierra Nevada are wonderful, particularly in the late afternoon.

Where the Vega meets the slopes of the *secanos*, or dry lands, ahead of us stands the village of Zujaira. Lorca ascribed several of the poems written in these parts, and included in *Book of Poems*, to the 'Vega de Zujaira', almost certainly because he did not want to print the name of his own village. Why not? Because its name, Asquerosa, coincides, believe it or not, with an adjective meaning 'revolting' or 'disgusting'. The etymology of the place name, which has nothing to do with the adjective, is disputed. It is almost certainly from the Latin *aqua* (water), however, and may mean either 'abundant in water' (*acuerosa*) or 'sweet water' (*aguarrosa*). Some people maintain that the word derives from the Latin for bow (*arcus*) and that in old Spanish it would therefore have been pronounced 'Arquerosa', Asquerosa being a later corruption. The 'archers' theory perhaps finds some support in the discovery of Roman tombs in the village, which suggests that the place may have been a Roman encampment. At all events, the 'Arquerosa' derivation was the one that Lorca preferred. 'I'm in Arquerosa (as you can see we've changed the name),' he wrote to Melchor Fernández Almagro in 1921.

Manuel de Falla was amused by the debate about the name of Lorca's village. After a visit to the poet's family in the summer of 1923 with his sister, María del Carmen, he joked: 'We both often remember the magnificent hours passed in Ask-el-Rosa.'

In 1943 the name was changed to Valderrubio, which means 'Valley of Light Tobacco', a reference to the *tabaco rubio* (literally 'pale') that used to be grown widely in these parts.

We now return to the main road, with its backdrop of poplars, turn right and then, almost immediately, swing left down another little track. To the right, a fine field stretches up to the edge of Valderrubio: it used to belong, all of it, to Lorca's father. I suggest that we be ecological and park the car here. Our next destination is only a few minutes away on foot down the path.

After about half a kilometre we arrive, on our left, at the spot known as the Fuente de la Teja (Spring of the Tile), beside the Cubillas. It has a little green gate and flower beds. This is a place of poplars, shade, warblers in the undergrowth, frogs, moorhens, peace. Lorca often came here as a child, alone or with companions from the village, and continued the habit when, later, his family used to spend part of their summers in Asquerosa.

This is just the nook in which to read, or re-read, the early 'Vega de Zujaira' poems, and *Suites* (a book Lorca never got around to publishing and which has been assembled from the manuscripts by the French Lorca authority, André Belamich). In the prose piece 'Meditaciones y alegorías del agua' ('Meditations and Allegories of the Water'), dated 1921, there is a direct allusion to the Fuente de la Teja, where, the poet tells us, he has been coming in the summer for many years. Bee-eaters, the breeze among the poplars, the frenzied grating of the cicadas, the depths of the green pool, the weeping-willows next to 'the tongue of the water' (in his lecture on Góngora, Lorca tells us that he once heard a peasant in Granada say: 'The willows always like to be in the *tongue* of the river'), the reeds, the ripples – here, 'on the cool bank of a river', Lorca's imagination took wing and he felt himself part of the world of water in its myriad manifestations.

In *Book of Poems* and *Suites* the poet's beloved poplars (*chopos* and *álamos*), inseparable in his mind from the banks of the Cubillas, appear over and over again, as they do in the letters of the period. Writing to Melchor Fernández Almagro that same year of 1921 he expressed his joy at finding himself again in the Vega after his recent period in Madrid. Here, he said, among these 'musical poplars and lyrical rivers', he had regained his peace of mind and could forget the passions which 'in the tower of the city attack me like a flock of panthers'.

The painter Gregorio Prieto received similar confidences. Greeting him from 'this magnificent Granadine Vega', Lorca said he was 'surrounded by poplars, river and clear, transparent sky'.

What moons preside over the Vega in summer! Lorca, a lunar poet if ever there was one, used to go into raptures over them. 'The other night a green and purple moon rose over the blue mists on the Sierra Nevada,' he told Adolfo Salazar, enthusing in another letter to the musicologist about 'the nights of full turquoise moon in the Vega'.

Returning to the car we now drive the short distance to Lorca's second village, bearing left as we enter it and seeing the church on our right. On its wall is a plaque commemorating the ceremony at which, on 15 August 1943, with all due solemnity, the village was named Valderrubio. As you will see, there is not the slightest reference to the place's previous, 'revolting', name. It's as if the village had been born that day in 1943, springing from nothing. But the old term survives and will do so eternally, thanks to the fact that Lorca lived and wrote here.

When the García Lorcas moved to Asquerosa from Fuente Vaqueros they lived first in Calle Ancha (today Calle Real), which runs down the side of the church. Their house was the one just beyond the latter, opposite that belonging to Frasquita Alba, prototype of Lorca's Bernarda Alba.

Frasquita Alba was born in 1858 (a year before Lorca's father) and had a son and two daughters by her first marriage. When her husband died she married again, in 1893. Alejandro Rodríguez Capilla was seven years older than Frasquita. By him she had four more children: three daughters and a son. The latter, Alejandro like his father, was the same age as Lorca and for a time his classmate in the village school. Frasquita died in 1924 and her husband in 1925. While she is still remembered in the village as a woman of domineering personality, she could at no time have ruled as a widow over the children of both marriages, as the dates show. Bernarda Alba's widowhood tyranny, then, was invented by the poet.

Lorca was fascinated as a child by the gossip about the Albas transmitted to him by Mercedes Delgado García, another of his favourite cousins, who lived next door. The Albas and Delgados shared a well at the back of their respective houses which was divided in half by the corral wall. Through the gap everything said on one side was clearly audible on the other, and Mercedes and her brothers and sisters always knew what was going on in their neighbours' house.

One of the daughters of Frasquita Alba's first marriage, Amelia, had married José Benavides, from the village of Romilla (which we saw behind the Torre de Roma), whose inhabitants are called *romanos*. When Amelia died, Benavides, known familiarly in Asquerosa as 'Pepico el de Roma', married her sister Consuelo. This was the seed from which Lorca developed the pervasive role of Pepe el Romano in *The House of Bernarda Alba*.

There are other borrowings from local life in the play: the dialogue, which reflects Asquerosa speech, lively despite the rather introspective character of the village compared to Fuente Vaqueros; the incredibly long periods of mourning which it was customary to observe here, hardly exaggerated by Lorca; the eyes watching from behind the curtains; the curiosity about sexual scandal; the arrival of the reapers each summer from the hills around the Vega, an annual event much looked forward to by the village girls; and the pitiless heat that beats down on Valderrubio in summer.

As in all Lorca's work, however, the 'facts' serve simply as the starting point. Bernarda Alba is a grotesque magnification of Frasquita Alba, and it is not surprising that the poet's mother should have begged him to change her surname so as not to offend the family. Had he lived to see the play performed, perhaps Lorca would have accepted this advice, although the loss would have been considerable, given the symbolic connotations of the name (a learned adjective for 'white') which are developed throughout his tragedy.

It cannot have been by chance that Lorca wrote a play on the theme of despotism at a time when anyone with any sense knew that there was a distinct possibility of a right-wing *coup* in Spain. Bernarda, with her hypocrisy, her inquisitorial Catholicism and her determination to suppress other people's freedom, represents a mentality known only too well to the poet. In calling the play *The House of Bernarda Alba*, moreover, Lorca put the emphasis on the environment within which the tyrant moves and has her being, making this intention explicit in the subtitle: 'A Drama of Women in the Villages of Spain'. When he termed the play 'a photographic documentary' the poet was indicating that it constituted a sort of contemporary report, with black-and-white illustrations, on reactionary Spain. 'The poor are like animals,' Bernarda pronounces. 'They seem to be made of different materials from the rest of us.' Writing out of his own experience of the Spanish countryside, Lorca was bitterly aware of the failure of the agrarian reform promised by the Republic – a reform initiated during the first two years of progressive rule, paralysed when the Right came to power in 1933 and yet to be implemented in June 1936, when he finished the play.

It seems likely to me, finally, that Lorca had his father in mind as he wrote the play. Federico García Rodríguez was probably the only powerful landowner in Asquerosa who professed democratic and Republican ideas. He had had several brushes over the years with his peers, and was disliked because he paid his men better than they did and had even gone to the extent of building houses for them. Such generosity was unheard of in the area and explains why in the village there is a street named after the benevolent patriarch. Don Federico was the 'good' local landowner, while Bernarda Alba is precisely the opposite. The play, on one level, is an oblique homage to the poet's father.

It should be added that, when the Fascists went to look for Lorca at the Huerta de San Vicente, some of the men were from Asquerosa and objected to the democratically-minded Don Federico García Rodríguez almost as much as to his poet son (see p. 91). I go into this matter in more detail in my book on the death of Lorca.

Soon after arriving in the village, the family moved to the nearby Calle Iglesia, No. 20, which Don Federico had bought in 1895. The street runs out of the plaza in front of the church at right-angles to Calle Real, and the García Lorcas' house is on the right. Today it houses the office of the local branch of the Socialist Party.

The patio behind the house bears little resemblance to the one that Lorca knew, which used to have a garden with flowers, trees and bushes. I feel certain that in the wonderful poem '1910 (Intermedio)', written in New York, Lorca is remembering that garden 'where the cats ate the frogs', and at the bottom of which, in the stable – or so the neighbours have assured me – several bulls used for ploughing were kept. This may explain the reference, among the memories of the house contained in the poem, to 'the snout of the bull'. The date of the poem's title is also significant. While the García Lorcas moved to Granada in 1909, Lorca always stated that his separation from his childhood paradise occurred in 1910 (he used also to claim that he had been born in 1900, not 1898). For me this is one of his most moving poems: the little village deep in the Granadine Vega recalled nostalgically from the heart of the American metropolis.

We know very little, really, about Lorca's two or three years here before the family moved to Granada in 1909. To my knowledge he never wrote anything about his experiences at the village school, for example, or about his companions. All of which, as his biographer, I found extremely frustrating.

At the end of Calle de la Iglesia we take the road to Láchar to visit the estate of Daimuz Bajo (Lower Daimuz), bought by Federico García Rodríguez in 1895, the same year that he acquired the house we have just visited.

At almost exactly one kilometre from the edge of the village we cross a dry gully. Three hundred metres further on the road turns sharply to the left and then swings right. Here, just where the right-hand curve begins, a lane leads off across the fields. Please park the car and walk the rest of the way. To the left of the lane stands a white cottage with two cypresses in front. In the far distance rises the Sierra Nevada. In 300 metres we arrive at a spacious farmhouse. This is Daimuz Bajo.

Don Federico García Rodríguez planted Daimuz with sugar-beet and before long was one of the richest men in the community. The estate formed the basis of the family's wealth. Typically, Lorca's father purchased it thinking not only of the advantages to himself but with a view to bettering the lot of his eight brothers and sisters, among whom he distributed portions of land.

The estate is not as large today as it was when the young Lorca used to stay here, for it has been divided up several times since then. As for the house, it too has undergone changes, mainly because of a fire that occurred not many years ago. It would not have looked very different in Lorca's day, however.

Daimuz has a picturesque history. The name, according to Luis Seco de Lucena, a specialist in Granadine toponymy, means 'The Farm of the Big Cave' in Arabic. Another authority, Miguel Asín Palacios, says the word can mean 'cave, cistern or spot'. Perhaps 'cistern' is the best bet, since the house has a deep well. No one around here seems to know anything about a cave, and in such flat terrain one wouldn't expect to find one. After the fall of Granada in 1492, Daimuz passed to one of the Catholic Monarchs' admirals. Then, for centuries, it belonged to an aristocratic Granadine family. Francisco García Lorca, the poet's brother, has written that his earliest memories are of

Daimuz. The two brothers enjoyed poring over the deeds to the property and seeing how the names of the respective title-holders changed: Doña Sol, Don Lope, Doña Mencía. The oldest documents, according to Francisco, were in Arabic letters.

Daimuz's history began long before it was tilled by the Muslims, however, as Lorca recalled in an interview granted in Buenos Aires in 1934. Talking about his happy childhood in Fuente Vaqueros, he remembered an incident that had occurred on the family estate:

It happened round about 1906. Our land, agricultural land, had always been ploughed by old wooden ploughs, which hardly scratched the surface. But in that year some of the farmers acquired the new Bravant ploughs (I've never forgotten the name), which had been awarded a prize for their efficiency at the Paris Exhibition of 1900. I, inquisitive child that I was, used to follow our new, vigorous plough everywhere. I enjoyed watching how the huge steel blade opened a slit in the earth, a slit from which roots, not blood, emerged. One day the plough stopped. It had hit something hard. A second later the shining steel blade turned out of the earth a Roman mosaic. It bore an inscription which I don't recall, although for some reason, I don't know why, the names of the shepherds Daphnis and Chloë come to mind.

This, my very first experience of artistic wonder, is related to the earth. The names of Daphnis and Chloë also taste of earth and love.

But did this scene really take place more or less as the poet described it some thirty years later? Francisco García Lorca, four years younger than Federico, doubts it in *In The Green Morning*, his book on his brother, alleging that, if on the estate of Daragoleja, not far away on the right bank of the Genil, near Láchar, Roman remains had certainly been found by 1906, such was not the case with Daimuz.

The poet's memory – by all accounts amazing – had not played him false, however. A few years ago, after Francisco's death, the vestiges of a Roman farmhouse were turned up by the plough in Daimuz Bajo. Numerous Roman coins have been found on the site, almost all from the period of Constantine. Moreover, the Archaeology Museum in Granada, as was mentioned in Tour Five, has a charming, three-inch-tall bronze statuette of Minerva found in Daimuz Alto (Upper Daimuz), close by. It seems to me certain, therefore, that in evoking his first experience of 'artistic wonder' the poet was remembering a true event when, in a thrilling, unexpected way the ancient history of Andalusia had suddenly been made palpable to him. So the Romans had lived on this very estate, now belonging to his father, years before the arrival of the Muslims who, in turn, had named it Daimuz! It is difficult not to relate the experience, recalled by the poet so vividly, to the Andalusia he later assembled in his ballads: a mythical Andalusia whose personality is composed of elements as diverse as the Tartessian, the Roman, the Christian, the Jewish, the Moorish and the Gypsy.

Doña Vicenta, the poet's mother, loved to read aloud to the folk of Fuente Vaqueros, a large portion of whom were illiterate. Lorca recalled that here in Daimuz he heard his mother read Victor Hugo's *Hernani*, a work which deeply impressed him (the García family all loved Hugo and had a complete set of the great man's works).

In this marvellous landscape the future poet developed the love for Nature that was to be a vital element in everything he wrote. When I come here I always remember the 'Words of Justification' placed at the head of *Book of Poems*, words deliberately exaggerated but none the less sincere for that:

Regardless of its stylistic infelicities and its obvious limitations, this book will have the virtue, among others which I suspect, of reminding me constantly of my passionate childhood running naked through the meadows of a valley with a backdrop of mountains.

Returning to the square in Valderrubio we now take the road to Pinos Puente and Illora, which leaves on the left just after the church. A kilometre and a half outside the village on the left, just after the bridge over the railway, is the cemetery. Its main interest for the '*lorquista*' lies in the fact that here are buried Frasquita Alba and her second husband, as well as other members of the family. Their tombs are in the back part of the enclosure, to the right of the main path. You may need to ask someone the way.

From the entrance to the cemetery you will see that here we are in a transitional area between the *secanos* (dry lands), with their wheat and olives, and the green immensity of the Vega. In the 'Meditations and Allegories of the Water' (1921), quoted earlier when we visited the Fuente de la Teja on the Cubillas, Lorca shows to what an extent he was sensitive to this transition from yellow and ochre to green; from the arid to the humid. I cannot resist quoting the passage:

I was returning from the dry lands. Down in the hollow lay the Vega, swathed in its blue shimmer. Through the recumbent air of the summer night floated the fluttering ribbons of the crickets.

The music of the dry lands has a markedly yellow flavour.

Now I understand how the cicadas are made of real gold and how a song can turn to ashes among the olives.

The dead who live in these cemeteries so far removed from every-where must turn yellow like the trees in November.

Once we draw closer to the Vega it seems that we are entering a green fishbowl; the air is a sea of blue waves, a sea made for the moon, where the frogs play their multiple flutes of dry reed.

Walking down from the dry lands to the Vega you have to cross a mysterious ford which few people notice: the Ford of the Sounds. This is a natural frontier where a strange silence seeks to deaden two, contrary musics. If our spiritual retina were adequately constituted, we would be able to appreciate how a man walking down tinged with the gold of the dry lands turns green on entering the Vega, after having disappeared for a moment in the opaque musical current of the dividing line.

It took Lorca to perceive that dividing line, and to perceive it in terms of music. Standing here by the cemetery looking out over this breathtaking scene, one can see just what he was getting at. Years before I read the passage in question (the *Suites* had not yet been published) I had been fascinated by the way the dry edges of the Vega contrast with the sudden green of the fertile plain, instead of gradually merging. Now the poet had 'explained' it all to me.

Starting off again we soon come to the road that leads, on the left, to Illora (where the Wellesleys have their estate) and, to the right, to Pinos Puente. On the other side of the junction, 100 yards or so back among the olives, there was an estate called El Cortijo Colorao (Red Farm) on which stood, in Lorca's youth, a Moorish tower (presumably a watchtower on the lines of the Torre de Roma). It has since been demolished. They say in Valderrubio that this was the tower referred to by Lorca in his poem 'Madrigal de verano' ('Summer Madrigal'), dated August 1920, included in *Book of Poems* and ascribed to 'Vega de Zujaira':

> Junta tu roja boca con la mía,
> ¡oh Estrella la gitana!
> Bajo el oro solar del mediodía
> morderé la manzana.
>
>     En el verde olivar de la colina
> hay una torre mora,
> del color de tu carne campesina
> que sabe a miel y aurora . . .

> Join your red mouth with mine,
> Oh Estrella the Gypsy!
> Under the sun-gold of midday
> I'll bite the apple.
>
>     In the green olive grove on the hillside
> There is a Moorish tower,
> The colour of your earthy flesh
> Which tastes of honey and dawn . . .

The villagers claiming to be informed on the subject say that Estrella really existed, and that her surname was Maldonado. Whether Lorca knew her personally or had any relationship with her now seems impossible to establish. In the village I have found no trace of the girl or her family.

The road continues towards Pinos Puente between groves of healthy-looking olives and soon passes three villages so close together that they are virtually one: Zujaira, Los Alamos and Casa Nueva. When we reach the junction with the N-432 a kilometre or so ahead, notice the rocky hill to the left on the other side of the road. This is the Cerro de los Infantes, on whose flat top are the remains of the prehistoric fort of Ilurco, built before the Romans invaded Spain in 218 BC. We turn right, crossing almost immediately the River Velillos, a tributory of the Cubillas. We then quickly pass two petrol stations, one on either side of the road, and 100 metres further on turn sharp left up the road signposted to Tiena, Olivares and Moclín. (If you have no time for this part of the trip you can carry straight on, consulting the latter part of this chapter.)

The road first follows the delightful, fertile valley of the Velillos and then, after Tiena, twists up a steep mountain slope dotted with almonds and enters a belt of pines. At the top of the mountain, on the left, is a sign to a *mirador*, or vantage-point. From here the view is fantastic: the wide green expanse of the Vega with its villages and thick plantations of poplars; the Sierra de Elvira, at the edge of the plain; the olive-clothed hillsides closer to us and, in the distance, completing the picture, the heights of the Sierra Nevada.

From the other side of the *mirador* we obtain an excellent view of the village, walls and castle of Moclín, which stands on a steep hill dominating the valley leading down to the Vega. It is easy to appreciate from here what an important role the castle played in the defence of Granada. It was finally captured by Ferdinand and Isabella in 1486. The Catholic Monarchs spent protracted periods in Moclín with their court until Granada succumbed six years later, and expressed their affection for the place by donating to the newly erected church a standard with a picture of Christ that had been carried throughout the campaign against the last Muslim enclave in the Peninsula.

During the sixteenth century miraculous powers began to be ascribed to the much refurbished picture, and at the end of the seventeenth the cult was officially recognized by the Archbishop of Granada, 5 October being fixed as the date for honouring the *Christ of the Cloth* (*El Cristo del Paño*), as it had come to be called because it was said to have cured a case of cataracts, known at that time as the 'sickness of the cloth'. Little by little the notoriety of the annual festivity increased, and by the eighteenth century many people made their way to Moclín from throughout Andalusia at the beginning of each October. No one seems to know quite why the Christ of the Cloth concerned Himself with impotence and infecundity in general and female infertility in particular, but so it was – and the afflicted travelled every autumn to Moclín in search of alleviation.

As a child in Fuente Vaqueros and then Asquerosa, Federico must have been familiar with the processions that passed each year through the Vega on their way to Moclín, and Francisco García Lorca has stated, moreover, that a crude lithograph of the 'Most Holy Christ of the Cloth' presided over his and his brother's shared bedroom (we saw a similar print in the Lorca Casa-Museo in the village).

By the early twentieth century the pilgrimage had acquired a strongly orgiastic quality, and if many pregnancies ensued annually it was more as a result of human than divine inter-vention, hundreds of men from the surrounding villages partici-pating in generative activity. 'Cuckolds! Cuckolds!' the locals would shout as the processions passed, alluding to the erotic sport which, in the interests of obtaining progeny, the unfortu-nate husbands were expected to tolerate during the expedition.

It is not known for sure if Lorca ever visited Moclín during the pilgrimage, or, indeed, at any time. His brother states that neither he nor Federico ever set foot in the village, although one of the poet's earliest biographers, Marcelle Auclair, reports a comment on the picture by Lorca that suggests that he had indeed seen the original: 'If you look at it well you can see, under the thin coating that covers it, the hoofs and thick hair of a faun' (*Enfances et Mort de Garcia Lorca*, 1968).

Lorca talked to his friends in Madrid about Moclín. One of them was the composer Gustavo Pittaluga, who decided to write a ballet on the theme, based on a plot devised by the poet and the theatre director and writer Cipriano Rivas Cherif. Pittaluga finished his *La romería de los cornudos* (*The Cuckolds' Pilgrim-age*) in 1927, but it was not performed orchestrally until 1930 and, as a ballet, until 1933. Today it is virtually unknown.

The plot of the ballet is trivial and the tone festive: neither has much to do with *Yerma*. What is important is that, three or four years before beginning to consider writing a play on the theme of female sterility, Lorca had collaborated on a ballet inspired by the Moclín pilgrimage. The final scene in *Yerma* owes much to the orgies that took place in the village, and deeply offended the Catholic establishment when the play was put on in December 1934.

If you have time you should climb up to the church and have a look at the *Cristo del Paño*. See if you agree with the poet about the faun lurking underneath. The painting has been much retouched, but I think I can see what Lorca meant. The look of this Christ is far from reassuring.

After visiting Moclín, we return the way we came and, arriving back at the N-432, turn left in the direction of Pinos Puente.

Just before we enter the town note the two chimneys on our right in the Vega. The nearer of these belonged to the Nueva Rosario sugar-beet refinery, founded in 1905 (as the inscription on the chimney testifies), one of whose leading shareholders was Lorca's father.

We now bear left into Pinos Puente to see the Moorish bridge, probably built on the foundations of an earlier Roman one. It was here, it is said, that in February 1492 a messenger from Ferdinand and Isabella overtook Columbus as he was spurring away from Santa Fe after the Monarchs' refusal to finance his expedition. No sooner had he left the encampment than Ferdinand and Isabella changed their minds. 'It was in the nick of time,' writes Richard Ford in his *Handbook*, 'and even then he hesitated to plunge back into the heart-sickening intrigues. Had he proceeded on his journey to our Henry VII, that sagacious monarch, ever alive to maritime expeditions, would have listened to his scheme, and S. America would today have been English and Protestant: on such trifles do the destinies of nations turn.' The remark is in the best Ford manner.

Leaving Pinos Puente for Granada observe how the stark Sierra Elvira (once famous for its grey serpentine) sweeps right down to the edge of the road. Three kilometres further on, after a military establishment with sentries posted on its walls, stands the shell of another old sugar-beet refinery, La Vega, founded, as the date on its chimney indicates, in 1904 (a year before the Nueva Rosario). This was the last such factory in the Vega to close down, in 1983.

Twenty minutes later we are back in Granada.

Note

If your aim is to visit only Fuente Vaqueros, I strongly recommend that you take the N-432 to Pinos Puente and Córdoba,
leaving the main road about 10 kilometres from Granada where
there is a signpost to Fuente Vaqueros. The road – by far
the most picturesque route to Lorca's birthplace – immediately
crosses the railway line and plunges into the depths of the Vega,
with its poplar groves, fields of tobacco (and sheds for drying
the leaves), maize, irrigation channels and, to date, not many
new buildings, although an intrusive refrigeration plant had
sprung up on the right of the road on my last visit. Seeing this
landscape one realizes again to what an extent Lorca's world
derives from his childhood immersion in the Vega.

# TOUR TEN Sierra Nevada and the Alpujarras

*Distance: the round trip from Granada to the top of the Sierra Nevada, down the other side into the Alpujarras and back to Granada is about 220 kilometres long. If you decide not to risk the road from the Sierra Nevada to the Alpujarras (see below), you can reach the latter by taking the N-323 towards Motril, branching off to Lanjarón 37 kilometres from Granada.*

*Length: a day.*

*A recommendation: fill the car tank before leaving Granada, because there aren't many petrol stations on this route.*

*A warning: the unsurfaced road from the Picacho de la Veleta to Bubión in the Alpujarras is only practicable in late spring, summer and early autumn, being snow-bound the rest of the year. It is, luckily, an appalling road, very twisty and at times hair-raising. I say 'luckily' because, if it were good, it would be crowded with cars, and the environment would suffer accordingly. I'm hesitant to recommend this route, for ecological reasons as well as the others; if you have strong nerves and decide to go ahead, make sure that your tyres are in excellent condition. And don't say I didn't warn you!*

Granada is dominated by the towering Sierra Nevada, the highest mountain range in Spain. The Mediterranean is only 48 kilometres away as the crow flies, but until recently, with the advent of better roads, seemed much more distant. 'Granada, which sighs for the sea,' the *Poem of Cante Jondo* puts it. To be so close to the sea yet so cut off is one of the circumstances that defines Granada.

From the town the Picacho de la Veleta (the Peak of the Weathervane), with its jutting crown, appears to be the topmost

N

GRANADA

Pinos Genil

Aeropuerto
de Armilla

Suspiro del moro

N 323

Valle de
Lecrín

Lanjarón

a Motril

Cáñar

Carataunas

Pampaneira

Capileira

Bubión

Trevélez

S I E R R A    N E V A D A

Solynieve

Pico de
la Veleta

Mulhacén

Escala: 1/250.000

point of the Sierra. In fact, at 11,246 feet, it stands 250 feet lower than the more rounded Mulhacén to its left, which takes its name from the father of Boabdil, the last Muslim king of Granada.

I mentioned in Tour Four how the engineer Juan José Santa Cruz began the road that was to lead from Granada to the Veleta and become the highest in Europe, recalling that the eccentric and mountaineering British Consul, William Davenhill, strongly disapproved of the idea (see pp. 54–7). That Santa Cruz, having achieved his dream, should have been shot by the rebels at the beginning of the Civil War is another sad reflection on the character of the city.

Before Santa Cruz built his road, few *granadinos* ever made their way up to the Sierra. Those who did so regularly were the *neveros* (from *nieve*, snow), who earned their living by bringing blocks of ice down to Granada on the backs of mules. The Camino de los Neveros, their trail up to the high mountains, still exists. Both Richard Ford and Théophile Gautier used it to reach the Veleta, and exchanged courtesies with the *neveros*. There are allusions to it, too, in Irving's *Tales of the Alhambra*.

In the 1920s there was a group in Granada called 'Los Diez Amigos, Ltd' ('The Ten Friends, Ltd') who loved the Sierra Nevada and organized an excursion there each year. Once Lorca went with them. His friend Miguel Cerón recalled years afterwards that the poet, a clumsy walker, found the going hard and was terrified that he would fall down a gully.

The road to the Sierra (the GR-420) leaves from the Paseo de la Bomba, beside the Genil. There are two interesting museum pieces in the Paseo.

The first is a couple of yellow carriages from the Tranvía de la Sierra (Tram to the Sierra). The tram was the brainwave of Granada's great benefactor, the Duque de San Pedro Galatino, who built the Hotel Alhambra Palace. The work was begun by Juan José Santa Cruz in 1920 and the line was inaugurated in 1925. When I first visited Granada in 1965 the tram still plied the valley of the Genil as far as Pinos Genil. It was a wonderful trip. Now, alas, it is a thing of the past, a fond memory.

The second exhibit, on the roundabout at the end of the

Paseo, is a steam-driven, French-made engine from the sugar factory La Vega, which we saw as we returned to Granada from Pinos Puente.

About a kilometre from the beginning of the road to the Sierra is being built, on the left, a new 2-kilometre-long access to the Alhambra (see p. 32).

Some 5 kilometres from Granada we come to Lancha del Genil. Hereabouts a new restaurant called the Venta de Eritaña was opened in the 1920s where, on 8 March 1928, Lorca and his friends organized a banquet to celebrate the launching of their avant-garde magazine *gallo*, mentioned in Tour Four. In his speech, which was reported in *El Defensor de Granada*, Lorca paid homage to Angel Ganivet and spelt out what *gallo* represented: love of Granada, certainly, 'but with our minds fixed on Europe'. I have been able to find no trace of the Venta de Eritaña. No one seems to remember it, and I assume that it closed down soon after opening.

The road soon crosses to the left bank of the Genil. After Pinos Genil (2310 feet above sea level) it begins to climb steeply, and splendid views open up.

After approximately 22 kilometres we see below the road on our left the Hotel Santa Cruz, a reminder of the man who wanted people to be able to drive up to the Veleta.

From kilometre 31 onwards we begin to see that William Davenhill's misgivings about Santa Cruz's project were well-founded. The development of the Sierra Nevada as a ski resort has produced Goyaesque horrors. Behold Solynieve, its buildings, its ski lift, its cars and its noise, and imagine what this is doing to the ecosystem, unique to the world. Not content with what has already been achieved, the developers want to make it all bigger and better and more glamorous. Here, in 1995, will be held the World Ski Championships. The consequences may prove fatal.

Continue to the Veleta. The last stages have to be negotiated on foot. If you're lucky you'll be able to see Africa from here (personally I have never been so fortunate). There is a wonderful description of the view in Angel Ganivet's novel *Los trabajos del infatigable creador Pío Cid* ('The Trials of the Indefatigable

Creator Pío Cid'), which Lorca must surely have known. Théophile Gautier's description is also first-rate. As for my hero Richard Ford, well, he devotes two wonderful columns of his *Handbook* to the ascent of the Sierra, which he did twice. While claiming that no pen could describe the view of sunrise obtained from the Veleta, his evocation of the daytime panorama from here is well up to his usual standard:

The *Picacho* is a small platform over a yawning precipice. Now we are raised above the earth, which, with all its glories, lies like an opened map at our feet. Now the eye travels over the infinite space, swifter than by railroad, comprehending it all at once. On one hand is the blue Mediterranean lake, with the faint outline even of Africa, in the indistinct horizon. Inland, jagged sierras rise one over another, the barriers of the central Castiles. The cold sublimity of these silent eternal snows is fully felt on the very pinnacle of the Alps, which stands out in friendless state, isolated like a despot, and too elevated to have anything in common with aught below. On this barren wind-blown height vegetation and life have ceased, even the last lichen and pale violet, which wastes its sweetness wherever a stone offers shelter from the snow; thousands of winged insects lie shrouded on that wreath, each in its little cell, having thawed itself a grave with its last warmth of life. In the scarped and soil-denuded heights the eagle builds; she must have mountains for her eyry. Here she reigns unmolested on her stony throne.

Three kilometres back down from the Veleta the road to the Alpujarras veers away to the left (there is a sign to Capileira). Forty kilometres of atrocious unsurfaced road stand between us and the village.

The excursion will prove unforgettable. The views of the mountains and glacial lakes are extraordinary, and the botanist will be in his element, even in high summer. Not so the ornithologist, though. Ford's profusion of eagles is no more, and on my last visit I saw no birds of prey, not even a pair of vultures.

Don't miss the Mirador de Trevélez, a signposted vantage-point that looks down on this, the highest village in Spain, famous for its cured hams.

I imagine that you will be relieved when eventually you reach the charming village of Capileira, with its Moorish-looking houses, and its sister villages of Bubión and Pampaneira.

When Lorca visited these parts, the road over the Sierra had not yet been opened, so he had to come via Lanjarón. At the beginning of 1926 he told his brother in a letter that he had just been to the Alpujarras in his friend José Segura's car, reaching to their 'very core'. The poet didn't mention Capileira, Bubión and Pampaneira – perhaps he didn't get this far – but says that in the next village down the valley, Carataunas, they told him that the Civil Guard had recently beaten up some Gypsies there.

A few kilometres down the road from Carataunas to Lanjarón, there is a spot on the right, just before the turning on the left to Bayácar, called Poyo Dios (God's Seat, presumably because the view is splendid). Near here the family of one of Lorca's friends, Rafael Aguado, owned an estate, the exact location of which I have been unable to identify. It seems that it was while visiting Aguado that the poet heard one of the locals sing the snatch of song that inspired his ballad 'The Faithless Wife':

Y que yo me la llevé al río
creyendo que era mozuela,
pero tenía marío.

And so I took her to the river
Thinking she was a virgin,
But she had a husband.

In the village of Cáñar, which can be reached by a steep road on our right a few kilometres further down towards Lanjarón, Lorca came to the conclusion that the Civil Guard were the true rulers of the Alpujarras. In the same letter to his brother he reported that here too they had told him about the barbarous behaviour of the guards, who had publicly beaten a fourteen-year-old Gypsy boy for the heinous crime of stealing five chickens from the mayor.

What Lorca heard about the Civil Guard's methods in Carataunas and Cáñar further confirmed him in his view of that body's role as the traditional enemy of the Gypsies. A year earlier, in 1925, he had already given poetic expression to the old vendetta in his 'Scene of the Lieutenant-Colonel of the Civil Guard', with its tail-piece 'The Song of the Beaten Gypsy'. As for his famous 'Ballad of the Spanish Civil Guard', it had been begun two years earlier and would be finished this year.

In Cáñar Lorca had seen 'washerwomen singing and sombre shepherds'. Today, however, the women of Cáñar have automatic washing machines and the latter-day shepherds, less sombre, watch TV when not looking after their flocks.

The poet found that the villages of the Alpujarras were very cut off from each other. There were hardly any roads. He told Francisco that he was pleased to discover that there were no longer any French or English tourists making 'lyrical trips' to the region. What he didn't know was that Gerald Brenan had already been living for several years in Yegen, a high Alpujarras village that Lorca almost certainly never visited. From Brenan's experience in Yegen would come one of his most delightful books, *South from Granada*.

Lorca convinced himself that in the Alpujarras there were two very distinct racial groups, 'the Nordic, Galician, Asturian type, etc., and the Moorish, which has survived intact'. 'I saw a Queen of Sheba removing the grain from maize,' he continued telling his brother, 'and a royal child disguised as a barber's son.' On the surrender of Granada in 1492, the Alpujarras were assigned by Ferdinand and Isabella to Boabdil. But the treaty was soon broken, and after the extermination campaign against the *moriscos* in 1568–71, led by Don Juan of Austria, Philip II's bastard brother, the survivors were dispersed throughout Spain and the area completely repopulated by Christians from the north – Lorca's *gallegos* and *asturianos*. None the less, some *morisco* families undoubtedly managed to hide and remain, while others may have found the means of filtering back into these valleys later before the final expulsion of 1609. Lorca, in other words, may not have been exaggerating excessively. See if you too can spot any Queens of Sheba or royal children masquerading as barbers' sons.

Lanjarón, the capital of the Alpujarras, is only twenty minutes down the road. It is an elegant, densely wooded spa famous for its curative waters and bottled mineral water. Lorca knew it well and often came here with his family. Doña Vicenta suffered from liver trouble and the celebrated water from the Capuchina spring apparently afforded her much relief (the spring is on the left of the plane-lined main street towards the end of the town coming from the Alpujarras). I have to confess that I find Lanjarón a bit depressing, with so many old folk carrying osier-encased jars of medicinal water. Have a look inside the spa; it's like travelling back to the nineteenth century.

In 1926 Lorca sent Manuel de Falla a postcard of the ruined Moorish castle, which stands below the town guarding the valley, and told Jorge Guillén that same summer: 'I'm in the Sierra Nevada and often go down to the sea in the afternoon. What a prodigious sea the Southern Mediterranean is! South, South! (admirable word south). Here the most incredible fantasies unfold logically and serenely.'

That sounds a bit like Surrealism and, in fact, Lanjarón is the most Surrealist town in the province. When Lorca returned here in the summer of 1927 after spending several months with Salvador Dalí in Catalonia, he was in a state of hypersensitivity that was increased by the hothouse atmosphere of the place. In a letter to his Barcelona friend Sebastià Gasch he wrote: 'I'm finding it almost impossible to sustain a normal conversation with the people here at the spa, because my eyes and my words are somewhere else – in the vast library whose books nobody has read, in the fresh breeze, in a country where things dance on one leg.'

Lorca was doing strange, surrealistic drawings at the time, freed of all logical control. He tried to explain to Gasch what was happening to him. His hand, he said, seemed to have acquired a sort of autonomy, casting itself out into the depths like a fishing line and bringing back a brilliant, unexpected catch of ideas and metaphors which formed themselves into rare shapes and lines on the paper. 'This dreaming isn't dangerous in my case,' he sought to reassure Gasch, 'because I have defences; it's dangerous only for the person who allows himself to be fascinated by the large, dark mirrors that poetry and madness place in the depths of their canyons. IN ART I KNOW

THAT I HAVE FEET OF LEAD. It's in the reality of my life, in love, in daily contact with others that I fear the chasm and the dream world. This, yes, is terrible and fantastic.'

Obsessed as he was at this time with Dalí, Lorca must have been forcibly struck by the fact that the patron of Lanjarón is St Sebastian, whose little chapel, with an unremarkable image of the saint, is just before the town, beside a petrol station, on the road down from the villages of the Alpujarras. Dalí and Lorca had been indulging for several years in secret games concerning the meaning of St Sebastian (unofficial patron of homosexuals and sado-masochists), and that summer Dalí had published his zany piece 'Saint Sebastian', which Lorca greatly admired, in the Catalan avant-garde magazine *L'Amic de les Arts*.

We can be certain that Lorca wrote frequently to Dalí that summer, although only one of these letters, and that a copy made in the 1940s, has come to light. It was sent from Lanjarón shortly after the poet arrived with his family, and hinges, almost inevitably, on the theme of St Sebastian. At the end of his letter Lorca is explicit about the extent to which he is missing Salvador. He complains that there is not a single well-shaped calf to be seen in the town, and that even the handsome waiters in the hotel cannot rouse his interest.

Have a look inside the Hotel España, where the García Lorcas used to stay during their visits. It's in the main street, at No. 42 (opposite the path down to the Capuchina spring), and has not changed substantially since pre-war days.

In a postcard of Lanjarón's 'Castaño Gordo', or 'Giant Sweet-Chestnut Tree' (which has since disappeared), sent that same summer of 1927 to Sebastià Gasch, Lorca insisted again on the African quality of the people and landscapes of the Alpujarras. 'Here one can understand the wounds of San Roque, tears of blood and the taste for knifing,' he wrote. 'Strange, Berber Andalusia.' San Roque (in French Saint Roch, in English St Rock) has a shrine in the town, which Lorca must have known. It is on the main street next door to No. 32. Inside is an image of the saint lifting his robe to reveal one of the wounds to which the poet refers.

The road outside Lanjarón on the way to Granada affords a fine view of the place's Moorish castle, as indeed it does of the wide and luminous valley on whose edge the town is perched.

Seven kilometres later we arrive at the main road from Granada to Motril. There are 37 kilometres to the capital and 25 to the famous knoll called the Suspiro del Moro, The Sigh of the Moor, thus known because it is said to have been from this vantage point that Boabdil, the last Muslim king of Granada, obtained his final glimpse of the city as he went into exile in the Alpujarras. Richard Ford again:

The banner of Santiago floated on his red towers, and all was lost. Behind was an Eden, like the glories of his past reign; before, a desert, cheerless as the prospects of a dethroned king. Then, as tears burst from his water-filled eyes, he was reproached by Ayeshah, his mother, whose rivalries had caused the calamity. 'Thou dost well to weep like a woman for that which thou hast not defended like a man'. When this anecdote was told to Charles V, 'She spake well,' observed the Emperor, 'for a tomb in the Alhambra is better than a palace in the Alpujarras'. Thither, and to Purchena, Boabdil retired, but not for long. He sickened in his exile, and passing over into Africa, is said to have been killed in a petty battle, thus losing his life for another's quarrel.

Two kilometres further on, just before the town of Alhendín, begins the controversial Granada bypass, finished in May 1991. If you are in a hurry to get back to your hotel, take it (there are several turn offs to the city). If not, carry on through Alhendín. After the town, on the left, note in passing the broad expanse of the military airport of Armilla. This airport played a role of prime importance in the Civil War, being one of the first objectives of the rebels when the rising began in Granada on 20 July 1936. They seized it immediately. The fighter planes that, on 22 July, attacked the workers resisting in the Albaicín took off from here; and it was from here that the Republican Military Commander of Granada, General Miguel Campíns, was flown to Seville shortly afterwards to be executed by the sinister General Queipo de Llano.

The city is now only 7 kilometres away.

In Dúrcal, on the road back to Granada, there is a splendid establishment, El Molino, an old converted water-mill where the Andalusian Centre for Gastronomic Research has set up an interesting museum and a restaurant specializing in traditional Granadine cuisine. Here you can sample a wide range of Moorish and later delicacies. If you want to eat, you will need to book in advance. The telephone number is: (958) 78.02.47. The address: El Molino, Paraje de la Isla, Camino de las Fuentes, Dúrcal (Granada).

# SOME PRACTICAL DETAILS

## INFORMATION BY PHONE
The Granada prefix (town and province) is 958.

All the telephone numbers given below are liable to be changed. You can check them by ringing Telephone Information in Granada as follows: (958) 03.

## CAR HIRE
Cars can be hired at Granada Airport, and should be booked in advance. At the moment of going to press the numbers are as follows:

Avis: 44.64.55
Hertz: 44.70.36

## TOURIST OFFICES
The main tourist office is in the Casa de los Tiros, Calle Pavaneras (opposite the Plaza del Padre Suárez). It is being refurbished at the time of writing. There is a temporary office in Calle Libreros, just off the Plaza de Bib-rambla, telephone 22.10.22, and another office at No. 10, Plaza de Mariana Pineda, telephone 22.75.13.

## HOTELS ON THE ALHAMBRA HILL
As I said in the introduction, try if you possibly can to stay on the Alhambra Hill. It's more pricey than down below, inevitably.

Four establishments can be particularly recommended, the first two being considerably more expensive than the others.

1. The Parador San Francisco, four stars, at the end of Calle Real de la Alhambra. Telephone: 22.14.40. It is described in Tour Three. The hotel has only 39 bedrooms and is almost always booked out well in advance. The manager, Don Juan Antonio Fernández Aladro, is a true lover of Granada.

2. The Hotel Alhambra Palace, four stars, No. 2, Calle Peña Partida, Alhambra. Telephone: 22.14.68. 144 bedrooms.

Whereas the Parador affords fabulous views of the Generalife and the Albaicín, the 'Palace' looks out over the city and the Vega. It and its Lorca associations are reviewed in Tour Four. If you stay here be sure you get a room facing the Vega. The manager, Don Gervasio Elorza, like his colleague at the Parador San Francisco up the road, is a man enamoured of Granada.

3. Hotel América, Calle Real de la Alhambra, three stars, a few doors down from the Parador. Telephone: 22.74.70 and 22.74.71. Shut between November and March. Here, too, it is usually necessary to book well in advance because there are only 14 rooms.

4. Hotel Washington Irving, three stars, No. 2, Paseo Generalife, Alhambra. Telephone: 22.75.50. About 80 bedrooms. The hotel, whose Lorca and Civil War associations are mentioned in Tour Four, is well situated beside the Alhambra Wood.

There are several more recent, but less interesting, hotels on the Alhambra Hill. They are all on the Avenida de los Alixares (the road to the cemetery above the Alhambra):

1. Hotel Alixares Generalife, three stars. Telephone: 22.56.06.

2. Hotel Doña Lupe, two stars.
Telephone: 22.14.73 and 22.14.74.

3. Hotel Guadalupe, three stars.
Telephone: 22.34.23 and 22.34.24.

BOOKSHOPS
For books on Granada, Lorca, etc., I recommend:

1. Librería Continental in the Puerta Real (technically, No. 2, Acera del Darro), just before Casa Enrique.

2. Librería Dauro, No. 3, Zacatín (leading out of the Plaza de Bib-rambla). This shop also deals in records and compact discs.

3. Librería Atlántida, No. 9, Gran Vía.

# SELECT BIBLIOGRAPHY

This brief list includes only titles in English. Any reader of *Lorca's Granada* conversant with Spanish is recommended to consult the bibliography appended to the original edition of the book: *Guía a la Granada de Federico García Lorca*, Plaza y Janés, Barcelona, 1989.

BIOGRAPHICAL ACCOUNTS OF LORCA

Francisco García Lorca, *In the Green Morning: Memories of Federico*, Peter Owen, London, 1989.
Ian Gibson, *The Death of Lorca*, Penguin, Harmondsworth, 1983.
Ian Gibson, *Federico García Lorca: A Life*, Faber and Faber, London, 1989; paperback, 1990.

EDITIONS OF LORCA IN ENGLISH

*Five Plays*, Penguin, Harmondsworth, 1990.
*Poet in New York*, translated by Greg Simon and Steven F. White, edited and with an introduction by Christopher Maurer, Viking, London, 1988. The Spanish originals are given with excellent English versions on the opposite page. These poems contain many allusions to the poet's childhood in Granada.

GUIDES TO AND BOOKS ON GRANADA

You should ask in the Granada bookshops mentioned in the section 'Some Practical Details', or elsewhere, what guides to the city are currently available in English. In Britain it should be possible to obtain the following titles:

Gerald Brenan, *South from Granada*, Penguin, Harmondsworth, 1961. Brenan's classic description of life in his village in the high mountain valley of the Alpujarras.
Washington Irving, *Tales of the Alhambra*, 1832. Another classic. If you find it's not available at home, an excellent English edition is published in Granada by Miguel Sánchez and constantly reprinted.
David Mitchell, *Travellers in Spain. An Illustrated Anthology*, Collins, London, and Lookout Books, Fuengirola, 1990. This beautiful book gathers together, among other good things, many interesting comments on Granada by English travellers who have sojourned in the city.

Carlos Pascual, *Granada*, in the 'Everything Under the Sun Travel Guide Series', Novatex, Madrid, 1988. You will find this slim-format, pocket-size guide extremely useful, not least for the street plans at the end.

# INDEX